Contents

Introduction

Welcome to the *Practice Test Pack for the TOEFL® Test*. This comprehensive resource for TOEFL® preparation provides you with practice, support, and knowledge about the test to help you succeed. The pack includes full-length tests, in both written and online format, to help prepare you for the internet-based test, the TOEFL® iBT.

What's in the pack?

The *Practice Test Pack for the TOEFL® Test* provides you with all the tools you need to succeed on the test. Here's a list of the learning tools included in this pack, followed by more detail.

- Access to four complete TOEFL tests online, and access to an interactive online training module
- A practice tests book containing two complete TOEFL® tests, a mini-dictionary, answer keys, and sample answers for the Listening and Speaking tests
- A complete guide to the TOEFL Test, with strategies for success and practical information about the test
- An audio CD with MP3 files

Practice Tests for the TOEFL® Test — This book includes two complete practice tests. Each test includes all four sections (Reading, Listening, Speaking, Writing) to allow you to experience the full exam as part of your study and preparation. (These two exams are also available online.) These tests include realistic test questions, showing you the types of questions you can expect to find on the test. Knowing what to expect is an important part of preparing for the test.

In addition to the practice tests, the book includes the **answer key** to the practice tests, the **audio script**, and **sample answers** for the Writing and Speaking questions. These tools will help you practice and check your answers as you prepare for the TOEFL test.

The book also contains a **mini-dictionary** of high-level words used in the practice tests, with definitions and examples to help you build your vocabulary. All definitions are from Collins COBUILD dictionaries.

Audio CD —This contains MP3 files for the Listening, Speaking, and Writing sections of the tests in the practice tests book.

Online practice tests —Access to four complete TOEFL tests online. Each test contains each of the four skills (Reading, Listening, Speaking, Writing). These online tests allow you to experience the conditions of the TOEFL iBT exam. By working through these four complete practice tests, you gain valuable experience of the online testing environment as you prepare for the test.

Online training module — The interactive training module allows you to take one of the tests in "training mode" and provides you with strategies for improving your skills on each part of the test, and additional practice. It also contains a step-by-step guide to what you will see on-screen when you take the test and detailed information on the TOEFL test itself.

The online tests give you the opportunity to practice taking the tests under exam conditions, that is, without interruptions or unscheduled breaks, and in a limited amount of time. It is recommended that as part of your preparation you take at least two of the practice tests under exam conditions.

Guide to the TOEFL® Test —This comprehensive guide presents you with strategies for success and essential test information. By using this guide you will feel completely confident about how the TOEFL test works, and know what to expect on the day of the test.

Specifically the guide contains:

- **Tips** for success — Best practice strategies and useful advice on how to prepare for the test and make the best use of the resources in the pack.
- A TOEFL Test **overview** — Use this as a quick reference to the TOEFL test whenever you need to remind yourself of specifics about test question types and what to expect on test day.
- **Quick guides** — Four quick guides present key information about question types for each test section in easy-to-read charts, making it simple for you to quickly understand what it is important to know in order to answer the questions correctly.
- Detailed, **step-by-step guides** to each part of the test that include explanations of question types, what correct answers must include, and how responses are scored.
- **Challenges and solutions** sections — These sections offer strategy and skill reviews to help you learn how to overcome the most common challenges on each part of the test.

Collins

English for Exams

PRACTICE TESTS FOR THE TOEFL® TEST

522 638 33 8

Collins

HarperCollins Publishers
77-85 Fulham Palace Road
Hammersmith
London W6 8JB

First edition 2014

Reprint 10 9 8 7 6 5 4 3 2 1 0

© HarperCollins Publishers 2014

ISBN 978-0-00-749970-0

www.collinselt.com

A catalogue record for this book is available from the British Library

Typeset in India by Aptara

Printed in China by South China Printing Co. Ltd

Photo credits:

p20: Toby Madden/HarperCollins*Publishers*; p22: Robert Kneschke/Shutterstock; p24: Alexander Raths/Shutterstock; p26: Toby Madden/HarperCollins*Publishers*; p30: bikeriderlondon/Shutterstock; p34: Toby Madden/HarperCollins*Publishers*; p37: Monkey Business Images/Shutterstock; p39: racorn/Shutterstock; p40: NotarYES/Shutterstock; p41: Corepics VOF/Shutterstock; p45: Golden Pixels LLC/Shutterstock; p76: Toby Madden/HarperCollins*Publishers*; p78: Diana Valujeva/Shutterstock; p80: bikeriderlondon/Shutterstock; p82: Alexander Raths/Shutterstock; p84: bikeriderlondon/Shutterstock; p86: Veronika Surovtseva/Shutterstock; p90: Toby Madden/HarperCollins*Publishers*; p93:michaeljung/Shutterstock; p95: ESTUDI M6/Shutterstock; p96: Monkey Business Images/Shutterstock; p97: tab62/Shutterstock; p101: Monkey Business Images/Shutterstock

How to use the pack

Studying the resources in the *Practice Test Pack for the TOEFL® Test* gives you the unique advantage of taking four complete TOEFL practice tests as you prepare for this important test. Because the test is divided into distinct skill sections, you will quickly discover where you need to focus your time in order to maximize your score as you work through the practice tests.

Once you have identified areas in which you need to improve, refer to the appropriate Challenges and Solutions section of the *Guide to the TOEFL® Test* for strategies and solutions.

After you complete each practice test, check the answer key to see where you chose incorrect answers and in which areas you need to improve. Study the correct answers in order to understand why they are correct.

Accessing the online component

Please use the access code at the back of the book to register for access to the online component. This contains four complete practice tests and an interactive training module.

Be sure to make the best use of all the resources in the pack in order to be prepared and feel confident on test day. Good luck!

TOEFL® TEST 1

Reading Section

This section tests your ability to understand academic passages in English. The section is divided into separately timed parts.

Questions are worth 1 point except for the last question for each passage which is worth more than 1 point. The directions for the last question explain how many points you can receive.

There are three reading passages in this section. You should plan to spend **20 minutes** reading each passage and answering the questions about it. You should take no more than **60 minutes** to complete the entire section.

Reading Section Timing Guide		
Passage	**Number of Questions**	**Time to Complete Test**
Passage 1	13	
Passage 2	13	60 minutes
Passage 3	13	

PART 1: READING 1

Read the passage.

Benjamin Franklin

Benjamin Franklin, born in 1706 and died in 1790, was truly a jack-of-all-trades and master of many. As a statesman, he, and several notable others, contributed to the formation of the United States as a nation. He was the only person to sign all four key documents of American history: the Declaration of Independence, the Treaty of Alliance with France, the Treaty of Peace with Great Britain, and the Constitution of the United States. He served as a diplomat, often praised as the most successful one America has ever sent abroad. What is not as well-known, however, are Franklin's many contributions to science, education, and culture.

Longing to be his own master at 17, Franklin ran away from Boston to Philadelphia, then the largest city in the American Colonies. The story of his arrival is part of American folklore. Numerous tales describe the young runaway apprentice bravely marching down Market Street with only one Dutch dollar in hand, carrying a loaf of bread. After seven years of working for various printers, he began publishing *The Pennsylvania Gazette*, soon turning it into one of the most successful papers in the colonies. He explained that successful people work harder than their competitors. He is also credited with publishing the first newspaper cartoon as well as the first story with an accompanying map. Franklin achieved even greater publishing success than the newspaper with his *Poor Richard's Almanac*. Each issue included Franklin's clever and witty sayings, many of which preach the value of hard work and thriftiness. These sayings remain part of American speech. Famous ones include: "Early to bed and early to rise, makes a man healthy, wealthy, and wise." "A penny saved is a penny earned." "Lost time is never found again." "Guests, like fish, begin to smell after three days." "Three can keep a secret if two of them are dead."

Although he never sought public office, he was doggedly interested in public affairs. Observing the poor state of the colonial postal service, he agreed to become Philadelphia's postmaster in 1737. The British government, observing his competency, appointed him deputy postmaster of all the colonies in 1753, and he initiated many needed reforms. Constantly aiming to make Philadelphia a better city, he helped establish the first American Colony library, lending books free of charge. He also organized a fire department in response to the numerous fires overwhelming the city. He reformed the city police. He began a program to pave, clean, and light the streets. He raised money to build a city hospital for the poor, the first city hospital in the colonies. With others, he helped found a school for higher education that became the renowned University of Pennsylvania.

Franklin's contributions as a scientist and an inventor are perhaps his most noteworthy. He was one of the first persons in the world to experiment with electricity. Flying a homemade kite during a thunderstorm, Franklin conducted his most famous electrical experiment in Philadelphia in 1752. A bolt of lightning struck a pointed wire that was attached to the kite and traveled down the kite string to a key fastened at the end, resulting in a spark. Then he tamed lightning by inventing a lightning rod. As a result, he proved that lightning is electricity. He urged his fellow citizens to use this instrument as a "means of securing the habitations and other buildings from mischief from thunder and lightning." His own home, equipped with the rod, was saved when lightning struck. He knocked himself unconscious at least once and suffered electrical shocks while proving his hypothesis and developing his rod.

Other notable inventions include the Franklin stove, making sitting rooms twice as warm with a fourth of the fuel they had been using. People around the world appreciate his inventions, bifocal eyeglasses in particular. They enable both reading and distance lenses to be set in one frame. He encouraged the enactment of daylight-saving time so that people would use less candlelight. He also showed colonists how to improve acid soil by using lime. He neither patented his inventions nor made profits from them, claiming his inventions were for all. He appreciated the inventiveness of others and often stated he wished he could return to Earth in a hundred years to see what progress humanity had made.

Refer to the passages below and answer the questions that follow.

Benjamin Franklin

[1] Benjamin Franklin, born in 1706 and died in 1790, was truly a jack-of-all-trades and master of many. As a statesman, he, and several notable others, contributed to the formation of the United States as a nation. He was the only person to sign all four key documents of American history: the Declaration of Independence, the Treaty of Alliance with France, the Treaty of Peace with Great Britain, and the Constitution of the United States. He served as a diplomat, often praised as the most successful one America has ever sent abroad. What is not as well-known, however, are Franklin's many contributions to science, education, and culture.

Directions: Fill in the oval next to your answer choice.

1. The term "a jack-of-all-trades" in paragraph 1 could best be replaced by
   - (A) talented in many fields
   - (B) man of many athletic feats
   - (C) multi-faceted lumberman
   - (D) dedicated electrician

2. The word "key" in paragraph 1 could best be replaced by
   - (A) successful
   - (B) mandatory
   - (C) fundamental
   - (D) opening

3. A diplomat would most probably serve
   - (A) in scientific endeavors
   - (B) in another nation
   - (C) as the French ambassador
   - (D) in higher education

4. It is NOT stated in paragraph 1 that Franklin is remembered for his contributions to

(A) nation building

(B) schooling

(C) diplomacy

(D) the presidency

² Longing to be his own master at 17, Franklin ran away from Boston to Philadelphia, then the largest city in the American Colonies. [7A] ■ The story of his arrival is part of American folklore. Numerous tales describe the young runaway apprentice bravely marching down Market Street with only one Dutch dollar in hand, carrying a loaf of bread. After seven years of working for various printers, he began publishing *The Pennsylvania Gazette*, soon turning it into one of the most successful papers in the colonies. He explained that successful people work harder than their competitors. [7B] ■ He is also credited with publishing the first newspaper cartoon as well as the first story with an accompanying map. Franklin achieved even greater publishing success than the newspaper with his *Poor Richard's Almanac*. Each issue included Franklin's clever and witty sayings, many of which preach the value of hard work and thriftiness. [7C] ■ These sayings remain part of American speech. Famous ones include: "Early to bed and early to rise, makes a man healthy, wealthy, and wise." "A penny saved is a penny earned." "Lost time is never found again." "Guests, like fish, begin to smell after three days." "Three can keep a secret if two of them are dead." [7D] ■

5. The author mentions "The story of his arrival is part of American folklore." in paragraph 2 in order to

(A) support Franklin's mythological heritage

(B) suggest that the actual events are unknown

(C) highlight Franklin's music connections

(D) document the connection to Philadelphia

6. The word "apprentice" in paragraph 2 could best be replaced by

(A) adventurer

(B) criminal

(C) ingénue

(D) trainee

7. Look at the four squares [■] that show where the following sentence could be added to paragraph 2.

One need only examine Franklin and his accomplishments to support this belief.

Where would the sentence best fit?

(A) [7A]

(B) [7B]

(C) [7C]

(D) [7D]

8. Which of the following best restates the saying in paragraph 2 "Three can keep a secret if two of them are dead."?

    (A) People have difficulties keeping secrets.

    (B) If you want to keep a secret, tell only three people.

    (C) It's better to have three friends than two.

    (D) Don't tell a secret to a dying person.

[3] Although he never sought public office, he was doggedly interested in public affairs. Observing the poor state of the colonial postal service, he agreed to become Philadelphia's postmaster in 1737. The British government, observing his competency, appointed him deputy postmaster of all the colonies in 1753, and he initiated many needed reforms. Constantly aiming to make Philadelphia a better city, he helped establish the first American Colony library, lending books free of charge. He also organized a fire department in response to the numerous fires overwhelming the city. He reformed the city police. He began a program to pave, clean, and light the streets. He raised money to build a city hospital for the poor, the first city hospital in the colonies. With others, he helped found a school for higher education that became the renowned University of Pennsylvania.

9. The word "doggedly" in paragraph 3 could best be replaced by

    (A) minimally

    (B) animatedly

    (C) determinedly

    (D) domestically

10. Which of the sentences below most clearly expresses important information in the highlighted sentence in paragraph 3? *Incorrect* choices change the meaning or leave out important information.

    (A) Franklin encouraged Great Britain to appoint him deputy postmaster.

    (B) In 1753 Great Britain initiated a postal service in the colonies.

    (C) The British government reformed the postal service in the colonies.

    (D) Franklin improved and overhauled the postal service in the colonies.

[4] Franklin's contributions as a scientist and an inventor are perhaps his most noteworthy. He was one of the first persons in the world to experiment with electricity. Flying a homemade kite during a thunderstorm, Franklin conducted his most famous electrical experiment in Philadelphia in 1752. A bolt of lightning struck a pointed wire that was attached to the kite and traveled down the kite string to a key fastened at the end, resulting in a spark. Then he tamed lightning by inventing a lightning rod. As a result, he proved that lightning is electricity. He urged his fellow citizens to use this instrument as a "means of securing the habitations and other buildings from mischief from thunder and lightning." His own home, equipped with the rod, was saved when lightning struck. He knocked himself unconscious at least once and suffered electrical shocks while proving his hypothesis and developing his rod.

11. It is implied in the passage that

(A) Philadelphians installed Franklin's lightning rod

(B) Franklin spent most of his life traveling abroad

(C) Franklin's death was caused by his work with thunder and lightning

(D) due to its location, Philadelphia is a lightning-prone city

⁵ Other notable inventions include the Franklin stove, making sitting rooms twice as warm with a fourth of the fuel they had been using. People around the world appreciate his inventions, bifocal eyeglasses in particular. They enable both reading and distance lenses to be set in one frame. He encouraged the enactment of daylight-saving time so that people would use less candlelight. He also showed colonists how to improve acid soil by using lime. He neither patented his inventions nor made profits from them, claiming his inventions were for all. He appreciated the inventiveness of others and often stated he wished he could return to Earth in a hundred years to see what progress humanity had made.

12. The word "they" in paragraph 5 refers to

(A) bifocals

(B) inventions

(C) people

(D) sitting rooms

13. **Directions:** Read the introductory sentence for a summary of the passage below. Complete the summary by choosing the THREE answer choices that include the key ideas in the passage. Some answer choices are incorrect because they include ideas that are not presented in the passage or are not significant in the passage. **This question is worth 2 points** (2 points for 3 correct answers, 1 point for 2 correct answers, and 0 points for 1 or 0 correct answers).

The passage discusses the most important contributions Benjamin Franklin made to early American life.

Fill in the oval next to your answer choice. **Choose three answers.**

① Franklin's *Poor Richard's Almanac* is widely read today.

② Franklin's proof that lightning is electricity had far-reaching implications.

③ Franklin was among the American nation builders.

④ Franklin worked as a policeman, a librarian, and a fireman.

⑤ Franklin never sought public office.

⑥ Franklin's many inventions improved the quality of life for many.

Go on to the next page ➔

PART 1: READING 2

Read the passage.

Training the Brain

People who can accomplish unbelievable mnemonic feats, such as memorizing thousands of random digits in under an hour, claim they have normal brains and that they do not have photographic memories: a gift that some people are born with that enables them to remember anything and everything. Some of these memory superstars compete annually in Olympic-like World Memory Championships. What these athletes do utilize are techniques that anyone can incorporate into everyday life to train one's memory. In addition to using techniques, these competitors undergo serious training and practice.

The World Memory Championships begin with the competitors sitting at a table with two shuffled decks of cards. Each person will have exactly five minutes to memorize the order of both decks. These mental athletes, or MAs for short, can memorize the first and last names of dozens of strangers in only a few minutes or any poem handed them. Ed Cooke, a 24-year-old MA from England, explains that MAs see themselves as "participants in an amateur research program" trying to rescue the long-lost art of memory training. In the not so distant past, Cooke contends, culture depended on individual memories. Almost all of Cooke's mnemonic techniques were invented in ancient Greece. These techniques existed not to recall useless information, such as playing cards, but to carve into the brain foundational texts and ideas.

A study in the journal *Nature* examined eight of the people who finished near the top of the World Memory Championships. The scientists examined whether these contestants' brains were fundamentally different from everyone else's or whether these people were simply making better use of memorizing abilities that we all possess. The researchers put the MAs and control subjects into brain scanners and had them memorize numbers, photographs of people, and snowflakes. What they found surprised everyone. The brains of the MAs and those of the control subjects were anatomically indistinguishable. On every test of mental ability, the MAs scored in the normal range. One surprising difference between the MAs and the control group surfaced; when the researchers examined what part of the brain was being utilized during a memory activity, they found the MAs relied more heavily on regions in the brain involved in spatial memory.

MAs offer a simple explanation. Anything can be imprinted upon our memories and kept in good order, simply by constructing a building in the imagination and filling it with images of what needs to be recalled. Dating back to the fifth century, this building is called a Memory Palace. Even as late as the fourteenth century, when there were perhaps only a dozen copies of any text, scholars needed to remember what was read or told to them. Reading to remember requires a very different technique than speed reading. If something is going to be made memorable, it has to be repeated. Until relatively recently, people read only a few books intensively over and over again, usually out loud and in groups. Today we read extensively, usually only once and without sustained focus.

What distinguishes the great mnemonist is the ability to create lavish images on the spur of the moment, to paint a picture in one's mind so unlike any other it cannot be forgotten and to do it quickly. Using memory palaces—of course not actual buildings—contestants create memorized images. For example, take a deck of cards and recombine the pictures to form unforgettable scenes such as routes through a town or signs of the zodiac. One competitor used his own body parts to help him memorize the entire 57,000-word Oxford English-Chinese dictionary.

Any novice who wishes to train the mind needs first to stockpile palaces. By visiting the homes of old friends, taking walks through various museums, or compiling a collection of famous artists, one can build new, fantastical structures in the imagination. Then carve each building up into cubbyholes for memories. One mnemonist associates every card in a deck with a different celebrity performing a strange act. Another puts every card into a different exhibit at her favorite museum. In a short amount of time, one will notice improvement with remembering license plate numbers or shopping lists. In order to keep the skill sharp, MAs deliberately empty their palaces after competitions, so they can reuse them again and again and recommend that novices do the same.

Refer to the passages below and answer the questions that follow.

Training the Brain

[1] People who can accomplish unbelievable mnemonic feats, such as memorizing thousands of random digits in under an hour, claim they have normal brains and that they do not have photographic memories: a gift that some people are born with that enables them to remember anything and everything. Some of these memory superstars compete annually in Olympic-like World Memory Championships. What these athletes do utilize are techniques that anyone can incorporate into everyday life to train one's memory. In addition to using techniques, these competitors undergo serious training and practice.

Directions: Fill in the oval next to your answer choice.

14. The word "undergo" in paragraph 1 could best be replaced by

Ⓐ participate in

Ⓑ contemplate

Ⓒ transport

Ⓓ travel to

[2] The World Memory Championships begin with the competitors sitting at a table with two shuffled decks of cards. Each person will have exactly five minutes to memorize the order of both decks. These mental athletes, or MAs for short, can memorize the first and last names of dozens of strangers in only a few minutes or any poem handed them. Ed Cooke, a 24-year-old MA from England, explains that MAs see themselves as "participants in an amateur research program" trying to rescue the long-lost art of memory training. In the not so distant past, Cooke contends, culture depended on individual memories. Almost all of Cooke's mnemonic techniques were invented in ancient Greece. These techniques existed not to recall useless information, such as playing cards, but to carve into the brain foundational texts and ideas.

Go on to the next page ➔

15. According to paragraph 2

(A) mental athletes are all from England

(B) mental athletes are strangers to the competition

(C) ancient Greeks used memory techniques

(D) ancient Greeks memorized first and last names of strangers

[3] A study in the journal *Nature* examined eight of the people who finished near the top of the World Memory Championships. The scientists examined whether these contestants' brains were fundamentally different from everyone else's or whether these people were simply making better use of memorizing abilities that we all possess. The researchers put the MAs and control subjects into brain scanners and had them memorize numbers, photographs of people, and snowflakes. What they found surprised everyone. The brains of the MAs and those of the control subjects were anatomically indistinguishable. On every test of mental ability, the MAs scored in the normal range. One surprising difference between the MAs and the control group surfaced; when the researchers examined what part of the brain was being utilized during a memory activity, they found the MAs relied more heavily on regions in the brain involved in spatial memory.

16. The word "they" in paragraph 3 refers to

(A) snowflakes   (C) mental athletes

(B) memorized numbers   (D) researchers

17. The word "indistinguishable" in paragraph 3 could best be replaced by

(A) impressive

(B) similar

(C) eminent

(D) indescribable

18. According to paragraph 3, it is NOT true that mental athletes

(A) have brains that are fundamentally different from everyone else's

(B) score in the normal range of mental ability tests

(C) depend more on areas of the brain that control spatial memory

(D) have brains that surprised everyone

[4] MAs offer a simple explanation. [19A] ■ Anything can be imprinted upon our memories and kept in good order, simply by constructing a building in the imagination and filling it with images of what needs to be recalled. Dating back to the fifth century, this building is called a Memory Palace. [19B] ■ Even as late as the fourteenth century, when there were perhaps only a dozen copies of any text, scholars needed to remember what was read or told to them. [19C] ■ Reading to remember requires a very different technique than speed reading. If something is going to be made memorable, it has to be repeated. Until relatively recently, people read only a few books intensively over and over again, usually out loud and in groups. [19D] ■ Today we read extensively, usually only once and without sustained focus.

19. Look at the four squares [■] that show where the following sentence could be added to paragraph 4.

They were able to recall large amounts of information by storing information in such a structure.

Where would the sentence best fit?

- (A) [19A]
- (B) [19B]
- (C) [19C]
- (D) [19D]

20. Why does the author mention "speed reading" in paragraph 4?

- (A) To discuss a fouth century technique
- (B) To illustrate why people read a few books intensively
- (C) To explain the copies of texts fourteenth century scholars needed to recall
- (D) To contrast the type of reading done nowadays with that of earlier times

21. The author mentions fourteenth century scholars in paragraph 4 in order to

- (A) illustrate why the printing press was such a necessary invention
- (B) explain why these people needed to remember what they read or heard
- (C) contrast those scholars with those of the fifth century
- (D) provide evidence for the discovery of palace structures

⁵ What distinguishes the great mnemonist is the ability to create lavish images on the spur of the moment, to paint a picture in one's mind so unlike any other it cannot be forgotten and to do it quickly. Using memory palaces—of course not actual buildings—contestants create memorized images. For example, take a deck of cards and recombine the pictures to form unforgettable scenes such as routes through a town or signs of the zodiac. One competitor used his own body parts to help him memorize the entire 57,000-word Oxford English-Chinese dictionary.

22. The phrase "spur of the moment" in paragraph 5 is closest in meaning to

- (A) timetable
- (B) clock
- (C) fly
- (D) brain

23. It can be inferred from paragraph 5 that

- (A) there are 57,000 body parts
- (B) there is a variety of unforgettable scenes
- (C) memory palaces can be quickly forgotten
- (D) decks of cards build actual buildings

Go on to the next page ➜

⁶ Any novice who wishes to train the mind needs first to stockpile palaces. By visiting the homes of old friends, taking walks through various museums, or compiling a collection of famous artists, one can build new, fantastical structures in the imagination. Then carve each building up into cubbyholes for memories. One mnemonist associates every card in a deck with a different celebrity performing a strange act. Another puts every card into a different exhibit at her favorite museum. In a short amount of time, one will notice improvement with remembering license plate numbers or shopping lists. In order to keep the skill sharp, MAs deliberately empty their palaces after competitions, so they can reuse them again and again and recommend that novices do the same.

24. Which of the sentences below most clearly expresses important information in the highlighted sentence in paragraph 6? *Incorrect* choices change the meaning or leave out important information.

   Ⓐ Those new to memory training need to create multiple memory palaces.

   Ⓑ Stockpiling memory palaces enables those new to memory competitions to win.

   Ⓒ Training the mind happens when one is new to competitions.

   Ⓓ When one stockpiles in battle, one enters a memory palace.

25. The word cubbyholes in paragraph 6 is closest in meaning to

   Ⓐ black holes

   Ⓑ zodiac signs

   Ⓒ confined spaces

   Ⓓ playing cards

26. **Directions:** Read the introductory sentence for a summary of the passage below. Complete the summary by choosing the THREE answer choices that include the key ideas in the passage. Some answer choices are incorrect because they include ideas that are not presented in the passage or are not significant in the passage. **This question is worth** 2 points (2 points for 3 correct answers, 1 point for 2 correct answers, and 0 points for 1 or 0 correct answers).

   The passage discusses how mental athletes are able to memorize astounding amounts of data.

   Fill in the oval next to your answer choice. **Choose three answers.**

   ① Memory athletes create lavish images that they delete after competitions.

   ② Memory athletes need to remember what is read to them.

   ③ Memory athletes use memory palaces to help them recall memorized images.

   ④ Unlike memory athletes, most people today read without attempting to remember details.

   ⑤ Ed Cooke is 24 years old.

   ⑥ Techniques memory athletes employ can be used by average people.

PART 1: READING 3

Read the passage.

The Endangered Turtle

A 655-pound leatherback sea turtle has just been released by the New England Aquarium after aquarium staff rescued the stranded and injured turtle two months ago off a mud flat in Cape Cod. The aquarium turtle is actually considered underweight, for these turtles typically weigh around 1,000 pounds. Forty percent of the turtle's front left flipper was gone due to a recent trauma. Leatherbacks, who use their large front flippers to pull their bodies through the water, often lose part of them to sharks or other large predatory fish and can still survive while at sea. These endangered sea turtles are rarely found alive after stranding. The aquarium has handled only five leatherbacks from Massachusetts beaches in more than forty years, all of which died subsequently. This release is truly a miracle, for only two other leatherback turtles are known to have survived after coming ashore anywhere in the world. The turtle will be closely monitored in the weeks to come with a tracking device inserted under its shell.

The leatherback is the largest living turtle in the world. It is also the longest-living marine species ever to populate the world's oceans. Leatherbacks roam tropical and subtropical waters of the Pacific, Atlantic, and Indian Oceans. Finding this turtle as far north as Massachusetts is a rarity. They survived catastrophic asteroid impacts and outlived the dinosaurs; however, scientists question whether the animal will survive into the next decade. If these turtles that lived for 150 million years are allowed to vanish, scientists fear it will foreshadow the extinction of a host of other marine species. In 1982 the population was estimated to be about 115,000 adult females. In recent years, however, the number of nesting leatherbacks has been declining at an alarming rate, in excess of 95 percent. Historically, these turtles were captured not for their meat but rather for their eggs, considered a delicacy even today in many parts of the world.

However, with fewer leatherback turtles in existence today, the number of eggs to poach has also waned. What then are major causes in the decrease? Scientists blame fishing nets, beach erosion, entanglement in other ship equipment, and sea trash. In 1987 shrimp fleets alone captured 640 leatherbacks in their nets. The turtles have been decimated by a fishing technique known as longlining, in which vessels lay out 40-to-60-mile-long lines of vertically hanging baited hooks. The turtles get caught up and tangled in these hooks. In response, the United States made the use of Turtle Excluded Devices (TEDs) mandatory for all fishing fleets, but scientists fear that this restriction will not be enough to save the leatherbacks from extinction. In addition to fishing nets, the turtles become entangled fairly often in anchors, buoys, other ropes, and cables. Another problem is their preferred nesting sites. The leatherbacks favor open access beaches, possibly to avoid damage to their soft flippers. Unfortunately, such open beaches with little shoreline protection are vulnerable to beach erosion, triggered by seasonal changes in wind and wave direction. A presumably secure beach can undergo such severe and dramatic erosion that eggs laid on it are lost. The turtles have also been severely impacted by trash in the seas. Leatherbacks have mistaken floating plastic bags, plastic and Styrofoam objects, and balloons for their natural food, jellyfish. Ingesting this debris can obstruct their digestive organs, leading to the ingestion of toxins that reduce the absorption of nutrients from real food. Ten of thirty-three dead leatherbacks washed ashore between 1979 and 1988 had ingested plastic bags or other plastic material.

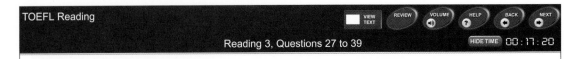

Reading 3, Questions 27 to 39   HIDE TIME 00:17:20

Saving the leatherbacks will take cooperation from nations around the world, for more than ninety percent of longline fishing takes place in international waters. Most nations, however, have taken steps to protect leatherback sea turtle nesting beaches in the last decade. Scientists are asking that all beaches where leatherback sea turtles are known to nest and lay eggs be protected and all egg harvesting be banned.

Refer to the passages below and answer the questions that follow.

The Endangered Turtle

[1] A 655-pound leatherback sea turtle has just been released by the New England Aquarium after aquarium staff rescued the stranded and injured turtle two months ago off a mud flat in Cape Cod. The aquarium turtle is actually considered underweight, for these turtles typically weigh around 1,000 pounds. Forty percent of the turtle's front left flipper was gone due to a recent trauma. Leatherbacks, who use their large front flippers to pull their bodies through the water, often lose part of them to sharks or other large predatory fish and can still survive while at sea. These endangered sea turtles are rarely found alive after stranding. The aquarium has handled only five leatherbacks from Massachusetts beaches in more than forty years, all of which died subsequently. This release is truly a miracle, for only two other leatherback turtles are known to have survived after coming ashore anywhere in the world. The turtle will be closely monitored in the weeks to come with a tracking device inserted under its shell.

Directions: Fill in the oval next to your answer choice.

27. Why is it mentioned in paragraph 1 that the aquarium sea turtle is 655 pounds?

   Ⓐ To foreshadow its subsequent release back into the ocean

   Ⓑ To illustrate its being endangered

   Ⓒ To explain why its flipper is gone

   Ⓓ To contrast its weight with other sea turtles

28. The word "predatory" in paragraph 1 could best be replaced by

   Ⓐ hunting

   Ⓑ historic

   Ⓒ irritable

   Ⓓ crafty

29. It can be inferred from paragraph 1 that the turtle has been inserted with a tracking device in order to

   Ⓐ follow its future movements

   Ⓑ watch it come ashore

   Ⓒ monitor its front left flipper

   Ⓓ measure its weight gain

30. The word "subsequently" in paragraph 1 could best be replaced by

(A) consequently

(B) underwater

(C) afterwards

(D) inexplicably

[2] The leatherback is the largest living turtle in the world. It is also the longest-living marine species ever to populate the world's oceans. Leatherbacks roam tropical and subtropical waters of the Pacific, Atlantic, and Indian Oceans. Finding this turtle as far north as Massachusetts is a rarity. They survived catastrophic asteroid impacts and outlived the dinosaurs; however, scientists question whether the animal will survive into the next decade. If these turtles that lived for 150 million years are allowed to vanish, scientists fear it will foreshadow the extinction of a host of other marine species. In 1982 the population was estimated to be about 115,000 adult females. In recent years, however, the number of nesting leatherbacks has been declining at an alarming rate, in excess of 95 percent. Historically, these turtles were captured not for their meat but rather for their eggs, considered a delicacy even today in many parts of the world.

31. The author mentions "They survived catastrophic asteroid impacts and outlived the dinosaurs; however, scientists question whether the animal will survive into the next decade" in paragraph 2 in order to

(A) compare sea turtles with their dinosaur ancestors

(B) emphasize the demise of the long-living sea turtles

(C) question whether the impact of asteroids led to sea turtle extinction

(D) calculate how many sea turtles will survive the decade

Go on to the next page ➔

³ However, with fewer leatherback turtles in existence today, the number of eggs to poach has also waned. What then are major causes in the decrease? Scientists blame fishing nets, beach erosion, entanglement in other ship equipment, and sea trash. In 1987 shrimp fleets alone captured 640 leatherbacks in their nets. The turtles have been decimated by a fishing technique known as longlining, in which vessels lay out 40-to-60-mile-long lines of vertically hanging baited hooks. [32A] ■ The turtles get caught up and tangled in these hooks. In response, the United States made the use of Turtle Excluded Devices (TEDs) mandatory for all fishing fleets, but scientists fear that this restriction will not be enough to save the leatherbacks from extinction. [32B] ■ In addition to fishing nets, the turtles become entangled fairly often in anchors, buoys, other ropes, and cables. Another problem is their preferred nesting sites. The leatherbacks favor open access beaches, possibly to avoid damage to their soft flippers. Unfortunately, such open beaches with little shoreline protection are vulnerable to beach erosion, triggered by seasonal changes in wind and wave direction. A presumably secure beach can undergo such severe and dramatic erosion that eggs laid on it are lost. [32C] ■ The turtles have also been severely impacted by trash in the seas. Leatherbacks have mistaken floating plastic bags, plastic and Styrofoam objects, and balloons for their natural food, jellyfish. Ingesting this debris can obstruct their digestive organs, leading to the ingestion of toxins that reduce the absorption of nutrients from real food. [32D] ■ Ten of thirty-three dead leatherbacks washed ashore between 1979 and 1988 had ingested plastic bags or other plastic material.

32. Look at the four squares [■] that show where the following sentence could be added to paragraph 3.

Without egg production, sea turtle extinction is inevitable.

Where would the sentence best fit?

Ⓐ [32A]

Ⓑ [32B]

Ⓒ [32C]

Ⓓ [32D]

33. According to paragraph 3, all of the following contribute to the decrease today of sea turtles EXCEPT

Ⓐ sea trash

Ⓑ anchor entanglement

Ⓒ egg poaching

Ⓓ beach erosion

34. The word "decimated" in paragraph 3 could best be replaced by

Ⓐ destroyed

Ⓑ injured

Ⓒ captured

Ⓓ tended

35. What is stated in paragraph 3 about why sea turtles prefer open access beaches?

   (D) The sites prohibit fishing nets.

   (B) The sites offer exposure to wind and wave direction.

   (C) The sites provide the natural food of the turtles: jellyfish.

   (D) The sites may offer protection for their appendages.

36. The phrase "vulnerable to" in paragraph 3 could best be replaced by

   (A) immune to

   (B) susceptible to

   (C) impregnable to

   (D) equitable to

37. The word "it" in paragraph 3 refers to

   (A) beach erosion

   (B) shoreline protection

   (C) wind and wave direction

   (D) a secure beach

[4] Saving the leatherbacks will take cooperation from nations around the world, for more than ninety percent of longline fishing takes place in international waters. Most nations, however, have taken steps to protect leatherback sea turtle nesting beaches in the last decade. Scientists are asking that all beaches where leatherback sea turtles are known to nest and lay eggs be protected and all egg harvesting be banned.

38. According to paragraph 4, why will international cooperation to save the sea turtle be essential?

   (A) Scientists from many nations regulate Turtle Excluded Devices.

   (B) US regulations alone are insufficient.

   (C) Sea turtle eggs are an international delicacy.

   (D) Sea turtle egg harvesting has been banned around the world.

Go on to the next page ➔

39. **Directions:** Read the introductory sentence for a summary of the passage below. Complete the summary by choosing the THREE answer choices that include the key ideas in the passage. Some answer choices are incorrect because they include ideas that are not presented in the passage or are not significant in the passage. This question is worth 2 points (2 points for 3 correct answers, 1 point for 2 correct answers, and 0 points for 1 or 0 correct answers).

Sea turtles are facing extinction.

Fill in the oval next to your answer choice.

Choose three answers.

1. US regulations alone are insufficient to protect endangered sea turtles.
2. Fishing fleets use plastic bags and Styrofoam to attract sea turtles into their nets.
3. Scientists from many nations use TEDs to regulate fishing fleets.
4. Sea turtle meat is considered a delicacy in many parts of the world.
5. Scientists fear that sea turtle extinction may signal that of other sea mammals.
6. Sea turtles become entangled in fishing lines, contributing to their demise.

STOP. This is the end of the Reading section.

Listening Section

This section tests your ability to understand conversations and lectures in English. You can listen to each conversation and lecture only **one** time.

After each conversation or lecture, you will answer some questions. The questions usually ask about the main idea and supporting details or about a speaker's attitude or purpose. Answer the questions based on what the speakers say or imply.

You can take notes while you listen. The notes may help you answer the questions. You will NOT receive a score for your notes.

You will see the **audio icon** 🎧 in some questions. This means that you will hear a part of the question that does not appear on the test page.

Questions are worth 1 point. If a question is worth more than 1 point, specific directions will tell you how many points you can receive.

You will have **60 minutes** to listen to the conversations and lectures and to answer the questions. You should answer each question even if your answer is only a guess.

PART 1

Questions 1–5

🎧 Listen to Track 1.

NOTES:

Directions: Fill in the oval next to your answer choice.

1. Why does the student go to the university office?

   Ⓐ To find his advisor so he can register

   Ⓑ To pay the library fine

   Ⓒ To sign up for the monthly tuition payment plan

   Ⓓ To have the financial hold removed

2. Which of these are true about the student's experience?

   Choose 2 answers.

   Ⓐ He cleared up the issue of the hold.

   Ⓑ He was told he had an academic hold.

   Ⓒ He is used to having his name mispronounced.

   Ⓓ He can't find his advisor.

3. Play Track 2 to listen again to part of the passage. Then answer the question.

   Why does the student say this?

   Ⓐ The student knows his last name is unusual.

   Ⓑ The bursar doesn't know who he is.

   Ⓒ The student can recall his ID number.

   Ⓓ The bursar can't pronounce his name correctly.

4. What must a student do in order to register for classes?

   Ⓐ Have his tuition bills disbursed monthly

   Ⓑ Not have any holds on his account

   Ⓒ Speak with the bursar

   Ⓓ Make sure to pay the ninety dollars

5. What will the student most likely do next?

   Ⓐ Go back to the library

   Ⓑ Discuss the payment option with his parents

   Ⓒ Look for his advisor

   Ⓓ Update his account with the university

Go on to the next page ➜

Questions 6-11

🎧 Listen to Track 3.

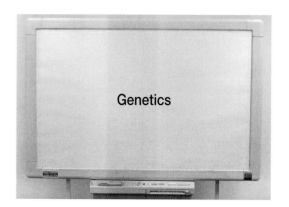

Genetics

pea plants

NOTES:

Directions: Fill in the oval next to your answer choice.

6. What does the professor mainly discuss in the lecture?

   (A) The explanation of why his wife has red hair

   (B) Mendel's personality traits and their impact

   (C) Mendel's theories and their applicability

   (D) Predicting the shape of garden pea plants

7. Which of the following are reasons the professor mentions for taking the course?

   Choose 2 answers.

   (A) To fulfill the science elective

   (B) To compare high school genetics coursework

   (C) To major in one of the natural sciences

   (D) To complete the final premed requirement

🎧 8. Play Track 4 to listen again to part of the lecture. Then answer the question.

   What does the professor mean when he says this?

   (A) That the students need to be paying attention to the lecture

   (B) That the students' memories may be damaged

   (C) That the students may have forgotten what he's about to discuss

   (D) That the students have too many things to remember

9. What are variants called?

   (A) Gametes

   (B) Genes

   (C) Offspring

   (D) Alleles

10. What does the professor say about red hair?

   (A) That if both parents are carriers for red hair but do not have red hair, their children will have red hair

   (B) That if one parent has red hair, the child will be red-headed

   (C) That redheads might die off in the near future

   (D) That it takes two carriers to have a red-headed child

11. What will probably be discussed in the next class?

   (A) The number of children the professor has

   (B) The hair color of the professor's wife

   (C) Gregor Mendel's hair color theories

   (D) Garden pea plants and their offspring

Go on to the next page ➜

Questions 12–17

🎧 Listen to Track 5.

NOTES:

Directions: Fill in the oval next to your answer choice.

12. Why does the professor want the class to visit Brook Farm?

   (A) To see the remaining cellar holes

   (B) To educate area children about the Transcendentalists

   (C) To learn about the Transcendentalists

   (D) To assist with a new Brook Farm project

13. What is true about the original Brook Farm?

   (A) It never had more than 15 members.

   (B) Nathaniel Hawthorne subsidized the community.

   (C) The members wanted to work the land.

   (D) The members rebuilt the site after the fire.

14. What is true about Transcendentalism?

   Choose 2 answers.

   (A) The spiritual world is the most important.

   (B) It includes literature as well as social issues.

   (C) It excludes social interaction.

   (D) It limits the number of community members.

15. Why was the professor contacted to promote the new Brook Farm?

   (A) Because he is a Transcendentalist

   (B) Because he has had farming experience

   (C) Because he is a Transcendentalist academic

   (D) Because he has student teachers in his class

🎧 16. Play Track 6 to listen again to part of the passage. Then answer the question.

   Why does the professor say this?

   (A) Teacher trainees can help with the neighboring children.

   (B) Teaching certificate students can get credit working there.

   (C) The new Brook Farm is looking for teachers.

   (D) His students will work in the area schools.

17. Which of the following is NOT mentioned as after dinner activities of the original Brook Farm members?

   (A) parties

   (B) outdoor physical activity

   (C) playing cards

   (D) singing

Go on to the next page ➜

PART 2

Questions 18–22

🎧 Listen to Track 7.

consultation

persuasive speech topic

NOTES:

Directions: Listen to a conversation between a student and a professor.

18. Why does the student go to see the professor?

(A) To practice his speech

(B) To choose between two topics

(C) To find an original idea

(D) To complete a quick survey

19. Which of these are true about the student's experience with the professor? **This question is worth 2 points** (2 points for 3 correct answers, 1 point for 2 correct answers, and 0 points for 1 or 0 correct answers).

Choose three answers.

(A) The professor suggests the student switch topics.

(B) The student needs to return during office hours.

(C) The student is still undecided on a speech topic.

(D) The student is reminded to include expert testimony.

(E) The student will present a week from Thursday.

20. What does the professor suggest the student do?

(A) Ask how many classmates vote

(B) Find a less academic topic

(C) Conduct an in-class survey

(D) Take a later shuttle to class

21. Play Track 8 to listen again to part of the discussion. Then answer the question. Why does the student say this?

(A) He is concerned that she may not get back to campus on the weekend.

(B) He thinks the professor may not be familiar with the shuttle system.

(C) He would like her to give him a ride back to campus on weekends.

(D) He needs her to know that students go downtown on the weekend.

22. What will the student probably do next?

(A) Have the class sign a petition

(B) Order new water bottles with logos

(C) Decide which topic to choose

(D) Practice his persuasive speech

Go on to the next page ➜

Questions 23–29

🎧 Listen to Track 9.

Directions: Listen to a lecture in an American history class.

```
NOTES:




```

23. **What does the professor mainly discuss in the lecture?**

Ⓐ The role of Frederick Tudor in building ice boxes

Ⓑ Utilizing ice in the refrigeration process

Ⓒ Events leading up to drinking iced tea

Ⓓ Home ice delivery by horse and buggy

24. Why does the professor most likely mention his grandparents?

    Ⓐ To honor their memory

    Ⓑ To personalize the topic

    Ⓒ To connect them with Tudor

    Ⓓ To insert an element of humor

25. What is stated in the lecture about Frederic Tudor?

    Choose 2 answers.

    Ⓐ He traveled to India.

    Ⓑ He was from Boston.

    Ⓒ He became known as the Ice King.

    Ⓓ His slabs of ice were for export only.

26. Match each description to the appropriate model on the right by placing a check mark (✓) in the correct boxes. **This question is worth 2 points** (2 points for 3 correct answers, 1 point for 2 correct answers, and 0 points for 1 or 0 correct answers).

    For each method check the corresponding column.

	Cheaper models	More expensive models	Refrigeration models
Used spigots for draining ice water from a catch pan			
Used electricity instead of ice			
Used a drip pan that was placed under the box			

27. Play Track 10 to listen again to part of the discussion. Then answer the question.

    How does the professor feel about the stories?

    Ⓐ They delighted him.

    Ⓑ He was bored by them.

    Ⓒ He was embarrassed by them.

    Ⓓ They became old.

28. In the talk, the professor describes the states in the history of refrigeration. Summarize the sequence by putting the stages in the correct order. Number each stage 1, 2, 3, or 4. **This question is worth 2 points** (2 points for 3 correct answers, 1 point for 2 correct answers, and 0 points for 1 or 0 correct answers).

    _____ Tudor sent ice ships from Boston to Calcutta.

    _____ Refrigeration began using electricity.

    _____ Tudor and Wyeth perfected an ice-cutting machine.

    _____ The icebox became a domestic necessity.

Go on to the next page →

Questions 29–34

🎧 Listen to Track 11.

NOTES:

Directions: Listen to a lecture in an economics class.

29. How is the information in the lecture organized?

(A) The causes of human behavior are clarified

(B) Various types of games are contrasted

(C) A topic is explained through an extended example

(D) The process is compared with another one

30. What is NOT mentioned as a type of situation that can be applied to game theory?

(A) a card game

(B) sports

(C) a military decision

(D) games of luck

31. What is stated in the lecture about game theory?

Choose 2 answers.

(A) All game theory games are reduced to board games.

(B) It is more complicated than it appears to be.

(C) It uses math to examine strategy.

(D) The players need to be people.

32. Are these statements true about the prisoner's dilemma? **This question is worth 2 points** (2 points for 4 correct answers, 1 point for 3 correct answers, and 0 points for 2, 1, or 0 correct answers).

For each sentence check the *YES* or *NO* column.

	YES	NO
If prisoners A and B stay silent, they go to jail for 6 months.		
If A betrays, and B is silent, B goes to jail for 6 months.		
If A betrays, and B is silent, A does not go to jail.		
If A and B betray each other, neither goes to jail.		

Go on to the next page ➜

🎧 33. **Play Track 12 to listen again to part of the lecture. Then answer the question.**

What does the professor mean when she says this?

- Ⓐ Since each country does not know what the other one will do, it should protect itself.
- Ⓑ Both countries always need to make weapons.
- Ⓒ Countries are like people, and sometimes they are altruistic.
- Ⓓ Countries need to study game theory before making weapons.

34. **Why does the professor mention what is called a repeated game?**

- Ⓐ To make clear that it is always the better strategy
- Ⓑ To explain why it is always better to betray the other player
- Ⓒ To indicate that in some circumstances players care about each other
- Ⓓ To show that participants will play the game a second time

STOP. This is the end of the Listening section.

Speaking

This section tests your ability to speak about different topics. You will answer six questions.

Questions 1 and 2 will be about familiar topics.

Questions 3 and 4 will include reading and listening passages. First, you will read a short passage. Then you will hear a talk about the same topic. Next you will answer a question about the text and the talk. Use the information from the text and the talk to show that you understood both of them.

Questions 5 and 6 will include part of a conversation or a lecture and a question. Use the information from the conversation and the lecture to show that you understood both of them.

While you read and listen, you can take notes that should help you answer the questions.

Listen carefully to the directions for each question. The preparation time begins right after you hear the question. You will be told when to begin to prepare and when to begin speaking.

QUESTIONS

Track 13

1. You will hear a question about a familiar topic. Listen to the question, and then prepare a response. You will have 15 seconds to prepare a response and 45 seconds to speak. You can take notes on the main points of a response.

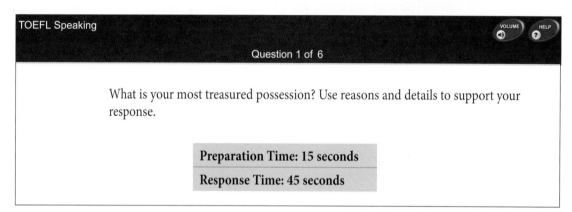

TOEFL Speaking

Question 1 of 6

What is your most treasured possession? Use reasons and details to support your response.

Preparation Time: 15 seconds

Response Time: 45 seconds

NOTES:

Track 14

2. You will be asked your opinion about a familiar topic. Listen to the question, and then prepare your response. You will have 15 seconds to prepare a response and 45 seconds to speak. You can take notes on the main points of a response.

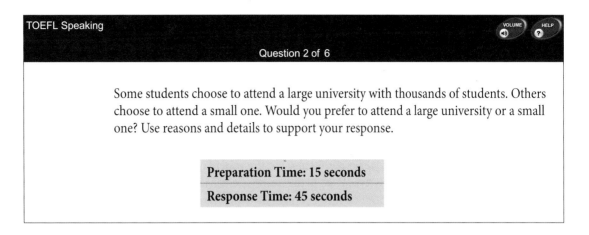

NOTES:

Go on to the next page ➔

Track 15

3. You will read a short passage and then listen to a conversation about the same topic. You will then answer a question about about them. You will have 45 seconds to read the passage. You can take notes on the main points of the reading passage.

Reading Time: 45 seconds

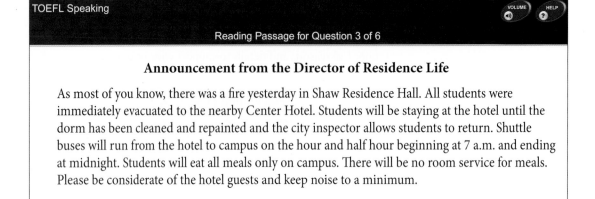

Listen to the conversation. You can take notes on the main points of the conversation.

NOTES:

Now answer the following question:

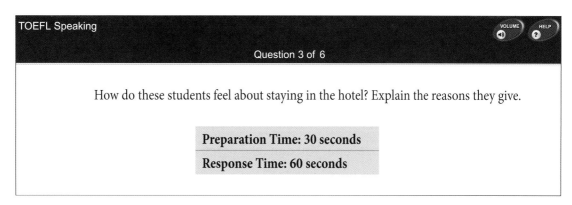

Track 16

4. You will read a short passage and then listen to a conversation about the same topic. You will then answer a question about about them. You will have 45 seconds to read the passage. You can take notes on the main points of the reading passage.

Reading Time: 45 seconds

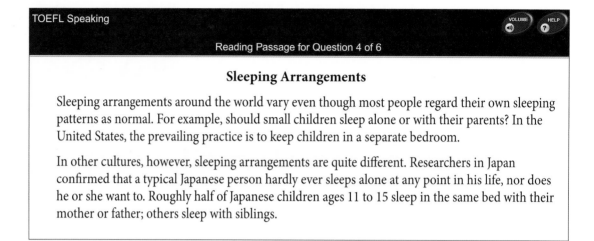

TOEFL Speaking

VOLUME   HELP

Reading Passage for Question 4 of 6

Sleeping Arrangements

Sleeping arrangements around the world vary even though most people regard their own sleeping patterns as normal. For example, should small children sleep alone or with their parents? In the United States, the prevailing practice is to keep children in a separate bedroom.

In other cultures, however, sleeping arrangements are quite different. Researchers in Japan confirmed that a typical Japanese person hardly ever sleeps alone at any point in his life, nor does he or she want to. Roughly half of Japanese children ages 11 to 15 sleep in the same bed with their mother or father; others sleep with siblings.

Listen to the passage. You can take notes on the main points of the listening passage.

NOTES:

Now answer the following question:

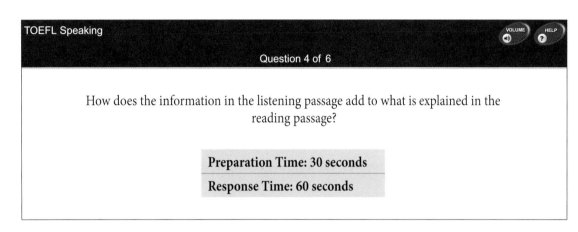

TOEFL Speaking

VOLUME   HELP

Question 4 of 6

How does the information in the listening passage add to what is explained in the reading passage?

Preparation Time: 30 seconds

Response Time: 60 seconds

Go on to the next page ➜

Track 17

5. You will listen to part of a lecture. You can take notes on the main points of the listening passage.

Now answer the following question:

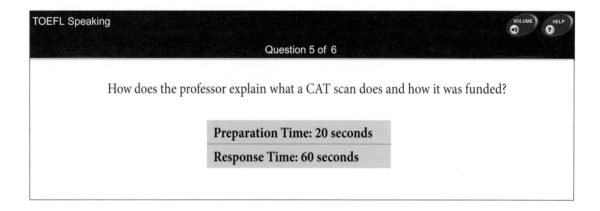

Track 18

6. You will hear a conversation. You can take notes on the main points of the listening passage.

Now answer the following question:

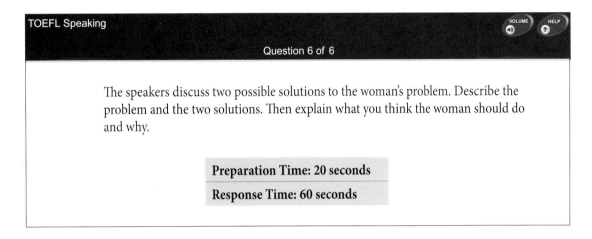

Question 6 of 6

The speakers discuss two possible solutions to the woman's problem. Describe the problem and the two solutions. Then explain what you think the woman should do and why.

Preparation Time: 20 seconds

Response Time: 60 seconds

STOP. This is the end of the Speaking section.

Writing Section

This section tests your ability to use writing in an academic setting. There will be two writing tasks.

In the first writing task, the integrated writing task, you will read a passage and listen to a lecture. You will then answer a question based on the reading passage and the lecture. In the second task, the independent writing task, you will answer a question using your own background knowledge.

Integrated Writing Directions

For this task, you will read a passage about an academic topic, and then you will hear a lecture about the same topic. You may take notes on both.

Then you will read a question about the connection between the reading passage and the lecture. In your written response try to use information from both the passage and the lecture. You will **not** be asked for your own opinion. You can refer the reading passage while you are writing.

You should plan on **3 minutes** to read the passage. Then listen to the lecture and give yourself **20 minutes** to plan and write your response. A successful response will be about 150 to 225 words. Your response will be judged on the quality of the writing and the correctness of the content.

QUESTION 1

Read the passage. On a piece of paper, take notes on the main points of the reading passage.

Reading Time: 3 minutes

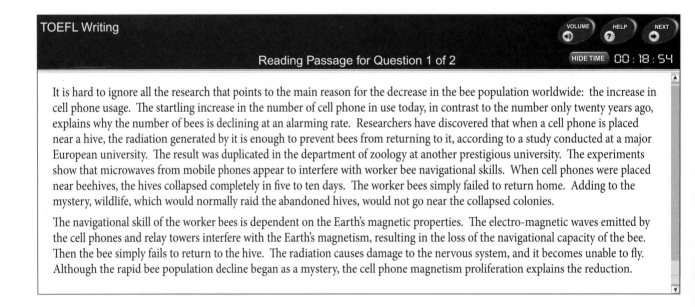

TOEFL Writing

Reading Passage for Question 1 of 2

HIDE TIME 00 : 18 : 54

It is hard to ignore all the research that points to the main reason for the decrease in the bee population worldwide: the increase in cell phone usage. The startling increase in the number of cell phone in use today, in contrast to the number only twenty years ago, explains why the number of bees is declining at an alarming rate. Researchers have discovered that when a cell phone is placed near a hive, the radiation generated by it is enough to prevent bees from returning to it, according to a study conducted at a major European university. The result was duplicated in the department of zoology at another prestigious university. The experiments show that microwaves from mobile phones appear to interfere with worker bee navigational skills. When cell phones were placed near beehives, the hives collapsed completely in five to ten days. The worker bees simply failed to return home. Adding to the mystery, wildlife, which would normally raid the abandoned hives, would not go near the collapsed colonies.

The navigational skill of the worker bees is dependent on the Earth's magnetic properties. The electro-magnetic waves emitted by the cell phones and relay towers interfere with the Earth's magnetism, resulting in the loss of the navigational capacity of the bee. Then the bee simply fails to return to the hive. The radiation causes damage to the nervous system, and it becomes unable to fly. Although the rapid bee population decline began as a mystery, the cell phone magnetism proliferation explains the reduction.

Play 🎧 Track 19 to listen to the passage.

Now answer the following question:

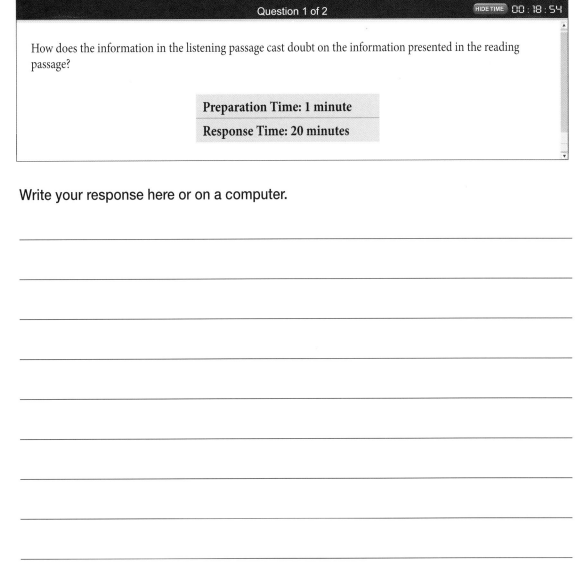

How does the information in the listening passage cast doubt on the information presented in the reading passage?

Preparation Time: 1 minute

Response Time: 20 minutes

Write your response here or on a computer.

_____

_____

_____

_____

_____

_____

_____

_____

Go on to the next page →

Independent Writing Directions

For this task, you will write an essay that explains, supports, and states your opinion about an issue. You will have **30 minutes** to plan, write, and edit your essay. You can take notes on the main points of a response.

A successful response will be at least 300 words. Try to show that you can develop your ideas, organize your essay, and use language correctly to express your ideas. The essay will be judged on the quality of your writing.

QUESTION 2

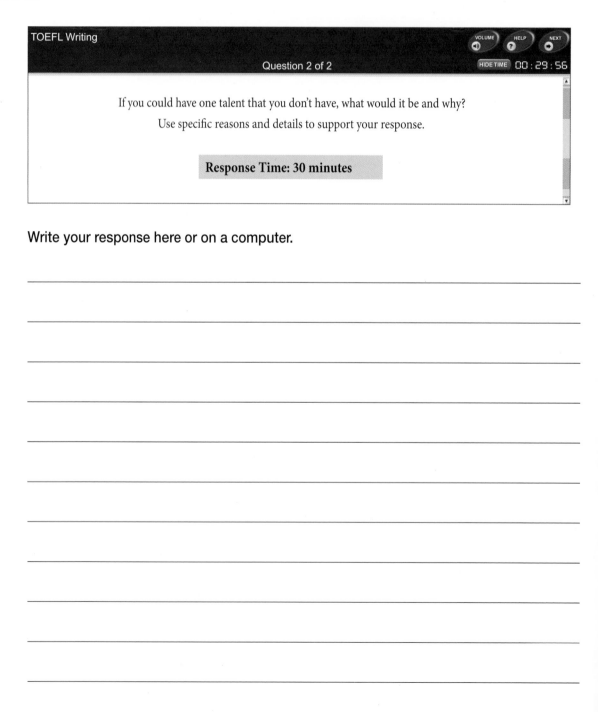

Write your response here or on a computer.

_____

_____

_____

_____

_____

_____

_____

_____

_____

Go on to the next page ➔

54

STOP. This is the end of the Writing section.

TOEFL® TEST 2

Reading Section

This section tests your ability to understand academic passages in English. The section is divided into separately timed parts.

Questions are worth 1 point except for the last question for each passage which is worth more than 1 point. The directions for the last question explain how many points you can receive.

There are three reading passages in this section. You should plan to spend **20 minutes** reading each passage and answering the questions about it. You should take no more than **60 minutes** to complete the entire section.

Reading Section Timing Guide		
Passage	**Number of Questions**	**Time to Complete Test**
Passage 1	12	
Passage 2	13	60 minutes
Passage 3	11	

PART 1: READING 1

Read the passage.

The French Encyclopedia

Neither Denis Diderot nor Jean d'Alembert were scientists. Living in the mid-1700s in France, Diderot was disowned by his father for wanting to become a writer and not entering one of the learned professions. Fortunately for history, Diderot followed his passion, for he and d'Alembert, ranked among the sharpest intellects of the day, fostered an environment in which earth-shattering discoveries could be made. They, and an army of experts and writers, published a set of encyclopedias about science, art, and trades in pre-revolutionary France.

Their encyclopedia began as a simple venture: a translation of a successful English work. Initially the two were writers, but once they advanced to be editors, they expanded the scope of the project to include all knowledge, not just literature. During the translation process Diderot's creative mind and astute vision transformed the original publication. Instead of a mere translation, the two collected the works of all the active writers as well as ideas and knowledge that were transforming the cultivated French population.

The first volume was published in 1751. This encyclopedia was unlike any other publication. The ideas expressed within its pages were unorthodox and quite progressive for the time. Diderot declared within the work his belief that there was a need for such an encyclopedia, and that it should include not only disciplines studied by the academies but every branch of knowledge. This was a revolutionary idea. In fact, the encyclopedia was one of the first works published during the Enlightenment. The Enlightenment was an eighteenth century philosophical movement stressing the importance of reason and the critical reappraisal of existing ideas and social institutions.

The encyclopedia comprised knowledge from scholars in the academies as well as knowledge of trades and business. The objective was to collect all knowledge of the time and present the information in a condensed form for all people to use. The encyclopedia covered different points of view, processes, and methods for its subjects. Reading these would be a means of betterment. This knowledge of various subjects would benefit individuals and society collectively.

Their encyclopedias contained numerous errors. Diderot and d'Alembert lived and worked in a time when printed material was anything but permanent. Rather than adhering to the original text, publishers themselves often changed the content depending on where the books were published and for what audience. Diderot felt disdain for some of the finished volumes. However, their primary belief, emphasizing observation over faith in traditional beliefs, remained intact. For example, they debunked a popularly held belief at the time that baby boys first utter the sound "A" while baby girls emit the sound "E." They devoted as much space to the manufacture of stockings as to the human soul. Needless to say, their books regularly came under fire, and Diderot had to spend some time in jail. The encyclopedias were plagued by controversy from the beginning. Just one year after the first volume was published the courts halted the project. But Diderot persevered, and the project resumed. Worn down by the constant controversy surrounding the encyclopedia, d'Alembert left the effort after the French government banned the work in the late 1750s.

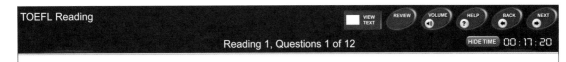

As the books gained in popularity, the government could no longer endure their influence and power. The encyclopedias threatened the governing social classes of the French aristocracy because it took for granted freedom of thought and the value of science and industry. The encyclopedias asserted that the main concern of the nation's government should be the nation's common people. The publication told the average man that he could know what only kings, emperors, and their lieutenants were supposed to know. It suggested that anyone should have access to rational truth. Although formally suppressed by the government, the decree did not stop the work, but it then was forced to continue in secret. Almost four hundred years since the encyclopedia's first publication, many credit d'Alembert and Diderot's work with fostering freedom of the press, the right for every man to vote, and the advance of science.

Refer to the passages below and answer the questions that follow.

The French Encyclopedia

[1] Neither Denis Diderot nor Jean d'Alembert were scientists. Living in the mid-1700s in France, Diderot was disowned by his father for wanting to become a writer and not entering one of the learned professions. Fortunately for history, Diderot followed his passion, for he and d'Alembert, ranked among the sharpest intellects of the day, fostered an environment in which earth-shattering discoveries could be made. They, and an army of experts and writers, published a set of encyclopedias about science, art, and trades in pre-revolutionary France.

Directions: Fill in the oval next to your answer choice.

1. Which of the sentences below most clearly expresses important information in the highlighted sentence in paragraph 1? *Incorrect* choices change the meaning or leave out important information.

   Ⓐ Diderot had to support himself as a writer.

   Ⓑ Diderot initially studied one of the learned professions.

   Ⓒ When Diderot lived, becoming a writer was atypical.

   Ⓓ In the mid-1700s in France one could not survive as a writer.

Go on to the next page ➜

2. The word "earth-shattering" in paragraph 1 is closest in meaning to

   (A) detrimental

   (B) categorical

   (C) consequential

   (D) disastrous

3. The word "they" in paragraph 1 refers to

   (A) discoveries

   (B) encyclopedias

   (C) Diderot and d'Alembert

   (D) of the learned professions

² Their encyclopedia began as a simple venture: a translation of a successful English work. Initially the two were writers, but once they advanced to be editors, they expanded the scope of the project to include all knowledge, not just literature. During the translation process Diderot's creative mind and astute vision transformed the original publication. Instead of a mere translation, the two collected the works of all the active writers as well as ideas and knowledge that were transforming the cultivated French population.

4. The word " venture" in paragraph 2 is closest in meaning to

   (A) trip

   (B) undertaking

   (C) expenditure

   (D) prank

³ The first volume was published in 1751. This encyclopedia was unlike any other publication. The ideas expressed within its pages were unorthodox and quite progressive for the time. Diderot declared within the work his belief that there was a need for such an encyclopedia, and that it should include not only disciplines studied by the academies but every branch of knowledge. This was a revolutionary idea. In fact, the encyclopedia was one of the first works published during the Enlightenment. The Enlightenment was an eighteenth century philosophical movement stressing the importance of reason and the critical reappraisal of existing ideas and social institutions.

5. The word "unorthodox" in paragraph 3 is closest in meaning to

   (A) unconventional

   (B) anti-religious

   (C) illogical

   (D) untruthful

[4] The encyclopedia comprised knowledge from scholars in the academies as well as knowledge of trades and business. The objective was to collect all knowledge of the time and present the information in a condensed form for all people to use. The encyclopedia covered different points of view, processes, and methods for its subjects. Reading these would be a means of betterment. This knowledge of various subjects would benefit individuals and society collectively.

6. Which of the following statements about the Enlightenment is supported by paragraph 4?

   (A) The encyclopedia contained scholarly works.

   (B) Common men worked in trades.

   (C) Information included alternative positions.

   (D) Knowledge of the time was condensed.

[5] Their encyclopedias contained numerous errors. Diderot and d'Alembert lived and worked in a time when printed material was anything but permanent. Rather than adhering to the original text, publishers themselves often changed the content depending on where the books were published and for what audience. Diderot felt disdain for some of the finished volumes. However, their primary belief, emphasizing observation over faith in traditional beliefs, remained intact. [9A] ■ For example, they debunked a popularly held belief at the time that baby boys first utter the sound "A" while baby girls emit the sound "E." [9B] ■ They devoted as much space to the manufacture of stockings as to the human soul. Needless to say, their books regularly came under fire, and Diderot had to spend some time in jail. [9C] ■ The encyclopedias were plagued by controversy from the beginning. [9D] ■ Just one year after the first volume was published the courts halted the project. But Diderot persevered, and the project resumed. Worn down by the constant controversy surrounding the encyclopedia, d'Alembert left the effort after the French government banned the work in the late 1750s.

7. The word "debunked" in paragraph 5 is closest in meaning to

   (A) questioned   (C) disproved

   (B) ridiculed   (D) investigated

8. Why did d'Alembert stop working on the encyclopedia?

   (A) Because he was forced to go to jail

   (B) Because the project was suspended by the courts

   (C) Because the unrelenting difficulties became tiresome

   (D) Because he was dismayed by the numerous printing errors

9. Look at the four squares ■ that show where the following sentence could be added to paragraph 5.

   When a factually incorrect belief is accepted as the truth, it is difficult to challenge it.

   Where would the sentence best fit?

   (A) [9A]   (C) [9C]

   (B) [9B]   (D) [9D]

10. The phrase "plagued by" in paragraph 5 is closest in meaning to

    (A) troubled by

    (B) ridiculed by

    (C) offset by

    (D) infested with

[6] As the books gained in popularity, the government could no longer endure their influence and power. The encyclopedias threatened the governing social classes of the French aristocracy because they took for granted freedom of thought and the value of science and industry. The encyclopedias asserted that the main concern of the nation's government should be the nation's common people. The publication told the average man that he could know what only kings, emperors, and their lieutenants were supposed to know. It suggested that anyone should have access to rational truth. Although formally suppressed by the government, the decree did not stop the work, but it then was forced to continue in secret. Almost four hundred years since the encyclopedia's first publication, many credit d'Alembert and Diderot's work with fostering freedom of the press, the right for every man to vote, and the advance of science.

11. It is implied in the passage that

    (A) Diderot and d'Alembert did not get along

    (B) the government believed the books would empower the common people

    (C) Diderot became a wealthy man from the sale of the encyclopedias

    (D) Diderot and d'Alembert's background in science and trades helped immensely

12. **Directions:** Read the introductory sentence for a summary of the passage below. Complete the summary by choosing the THREE answer choices that include the key ideas in the passage. Some answer choices are incorrect because they include ideas that are not presented in the passage or are not significant in the passage. **This question is worth 2 points** (2 points for 3 correct answers, 1 point for 2 correct answers, and 0 points for 1 or 0 correct answers).

The passage discusses the most important contributions The French Encyclopedia made to French life.

Fill in the oval next to your answer choice.

Choose three answers.

    (1) Due to the publication of the books, printing errors decreased.

    (2) The books declared the government should concern itself with common people.

    (3) Kings and emperors gave access to what they knew.

    (4) The average man gained access to rational truth.

    (5) The books condensed what was known about the world for all to use.

    (6) People were free to study what they chose, not what was expected.

PART 1: READING 2

Read the passage.

The Land-Grant College System

The history of land-grant colleges of agriculture in the United States is closely tied to the rise in higher education opportunities for children of working families. The land-grant system began in 1862 with a piece of legislation known as the Morrill Act. This act funded educational institutions by granting federally controlled land to all states for them to develop or sell to raise funds to establish and endow "land-grant" colleges. The mission of these institutions as set forth in the 1862 Act is to focus on the teaching of practical agriculture, military tactics, science and engineering, though without excluding classical studies, as a response to the industrial revolution and changing social mobility. This mission was in contrast to the historic practice of higher education to focus on an abstract liberal arts curriculum. The legislative mandate for these land-grant colleges helped extend higher education to broad segments of the US population so that members of the working classes could obtain a liberal, practical education.

Public universities existed already in some states, such as the University of Michigan founded in 1814; however, higher education was still widely unavailable to many agricultural and industrial workers. The Morrill Act was intended to provide a broad segment of the population with a practical education that had direct relevance to their daily lives. Most states responded to the Morrill Act by legislating new agricultural and mechanical arts colleges rather than by endowing already existing state institutions. The act gave rise to a network of often poorly financed colleges known as the 1862s. The Second Morrill Act, which provided for annual appropriations to each state to support its land-grant colleges, was passed in Congress in 1890.

The first land-grant bill was introduced in Congress by Vermont Representative Justin Morrill—hence the name of the Act—in 1857. After much struggle, the bill passed in 1859, only to be vetoed by President James Buchanan. In 1861, Morrill resubmitted the bill that increased to 30,000 acres the grant for each senator and representative and added a requirement that institutions teach military tactics. The need for trained military officers to fight in the Civil War, along with the absence of Southern legislators who had opposed the earlier bill, helped the Act sail through Congress in just six months. President Abraham Lincoln signed it into law on July 2, 1862. Iowa was the first state legislature to accept the provisions, designating the State Agricultural College, known today as Iowa State University, as the land-grant college in 1864. The oldest school to hold land-grant status is Rutgers University, founded in 1766 and designated the land-grant college of New Jersey in 1864.

Over the decades, as the US economy grew and changed, so did the nature of demands for education and scientific pursuit. As more and more US citizens began to attend college, most colleges of agriculture were transformed into full-fledged universities. In some states, like California, Maryland, Minnesota, and Wisconsin, land-grant universities have become the foremost public institutions of higher education and scientific research. In others, such as North Carolina, Michigan, and Oregon, higher education and research functions are shared with other prominent institutions. Ultimately, most land-grant colleges became large public universities that offer a full spectrum of educational opportunities. Only a very few land-grant colleges are private schools, including Cornell University and the Massachusetts Institute of Technology.

Although many land-grant universities are still known today for their agricultural roots, others have little agricultural identity and students are rarely from farm families. Today most of the land-grant colleges have expanded well beyond teaching only agriculture and mechanical arts and, therefore, are indistinguishable from other universities. The "colleges of agriculture" still in existence at land-grant universities resemble one another in their mission and curriculum. These universities continue to fulfill their democratic mandate for openness, accessibility, and service to people, and many of these institutions have joined the ranks of the nation's most distinguished public research universities. Through the land-grant university heritage, millions of students in each state and territory of the US are able to study every academic discipline and explore fields far beyond the scope envisioned in the original land-grant mission.

Refer to the passages below and answer the questions that follow.

The Land-Grant College System

[1] The history of land-grant colleges of agriculture in the United States is closely tied to the rise in higher education opportunities for children of working families. The land-grant system began in 1862 with a piece of legislation known as the Morrill Act. This act funded educational institutions by granting federally controlled land to all states for them to develop or sell to raise funds to establish and endow "land-grant" colleges. The mission of these institutions as set forth in the 1862 Act is to focus on the teaching of practical agriculture, military tactics, science and engineering, though without excluding classical studies, as a response to the industrial revolution and changing social mobility. This mission was in contrast to the historic practice of higher education to focus on an abstract liberal arts curriculum. The legislative mandate for these land-grant colleges helped extend higher education to broad segments of the US population so that members of the working classes could obtain a liberal, practical education.

Directions: Fill in the oval next to your answer choice.

13. The word "endow" in paragraph 1 is closest in meaning to

   (A) finance   (C) inhabit

   (B) name   (D) build

14. According to paragraph 1, it is NOT true that land-grant colleges were established in order to

   (A) respond to the Industrial Revolution

   (B) focus on a traditional liberal arts curriculum

   (C) include studies such as engineering

   (D) extend an education to the working class

15. The phrase "set forth" in paragraph 1 is closest in meaning to

   (A) strengthened   (C) proposed

   (B) postponed   (D) quadrupled

16. The word "mandate" in paragraph 1 is closest in meaning to

Ⓐ authorization

Ⓑ jurisdiction

Ⓒ donation

Ⓓ bill

2 Public universities existed already in some states, such as the University of Michigan founded in 1814; however, higher education was still widely unavailable to many agricultural and industrial workers. The Morrill Act was intended to provide a broad segment of the population with a practical education that had direct relevance to their daily lives. Most states responded to the Morrill Act by legislating new agricultural and mechanical arts colleges rather than by endowing already existing state institutions. The act gave rise to a network of often poorly financed colleges known as the 1862s. The Second Morrill Act, which provided for annual appropriations to each state to support its land-grant colleges, was passed in Congress in 1890.

17. According to paragraph 2, which of the following is true?

Ⓐ The Morrill Act created the University of Michigan.

Ⓑ Farmers had wide access to higher education before 1862.

Ⓒ Some states already had public universities in 1862.

Ⓓ The Second Morrill Act was passed in response to 1862s.

18. The word "its" in paragraph 2 refers to

Ⓐ land-grant colleges

Ⓑ The Second Morrill Act

Ⓒ each state

Ⓓ appropriations

3 The first land-grant bill was introduced in Congress by Vermont Representative Justin Morrill—hence the name of the Act—in 1857. After much struggle, the bill passed in 1859, only to be vetoed by President James Buchanan. In 1861, Morrill resubmitted the bill that increased to 30,000 acres the grant for each senator and representative and added a requirement that institutions teach military tactics. The need for trained military officers to fight in the Civil War, along with the absence of Southern legislators who had opposed the earlier bill, helped the Act sail through Congress in just six months. President Abraham Lincoln signed it into law on July 2, 1862. Iowa was the first state legislature to accept the provisions, designating the State Agricultural College, known today as Iowa State University, as the land-grant college in 1864. The oldest school to hold land-grant status is Rutgers University, founded in 1766 and designated the land-grant college of New Jersey in 1864.

19. The phrase "sail through" in paragraph 3 is closest in meaning to

Ⓐ circumnavigate

Ⓑ ignore completely

Ⓒ bypass entirely

Ⓓ pass easily

Go on to the next page ➜

20. According to paragraph 3, what contributed to the passing of the 1861 resubmitted bill?

    Ⓐ That President Buchanan vetoed the 1859 bill

    Ⓑ That teaching of military tactics was included

    Ⓒ That Southern legislators were fighting the Civil War

    Ⓓ That a total of 30,000 acres was added to the bill

---

⁴ [23A] ■ Over the decades, as the US economy grew and changed, so did the nature of demands for education and scientific pursuit. As more and more US citizens began to attend college, most colleges of agriculture were transformed into full-fledged universities. [23B] ■ In some states, like California, Maryland, Minnesota, and Wisconsin, land-grant universities have become the foremost public institutions of higher education and scientific research. In others, such as North Carolina, Michigan, and Oregon, higher education and research functions are shared with other prominent institutions. [23C] ■ Ultimately, most land-grant colleges became large public universities that offer a full spectrum of educational opportunities. [23D] ■ Only a very few land-grant colleges are private schools, including Cornell University and the Massachusetts Institute of Technology.

---

21. The word "pursuit" in paragraph 4 is closest in meaning to

    Ⓐ hunting

    Ⓑ occupation

    Ⓒ follow-up

    Ⓓ inquiry

22. Which of the sentences below most clearly expresses important information in the highlighted sentence in paragraph 4? *Incorrect* choices change the meaning or leave out important information.

    Ⓐ Some states share functions with other prestigious institutions.

    Ⓑ Some state universities were the forerunners of land-grant universities.

    Ⓒ In some states the land-grant universities are the flagship institutions.

    Ⓓ In some states there are full-fledged research institutions.

23. Look at the four squares [■] that show where the following sentence could be added to paragraph 4.

Most states chose to award land-grant status to public universities.

Where would the sentence best fit?

    Ⓐ [23A]

    Ⓑ [23B]

    Ⓒ [23C]

    Ⓓ [23D]

⁵ Although many land-grant universities are still known today for their agricultural roots, others have little agricultural identity and students are rarely from farm families. Today most of the land-grant colleges have expanded well beyond teaching only agriculture and mechanical arts and, therefore, are indistinguishable from other universities. The "colleges of agriculture" still in existence at land-grant universities resemble one another in their mission and curriculum. These universities continue to fulfill their democratic mandate for openness, accessibility, and service to people, and many of these institutions have joined the ranks of the nation's most distinguished public research universities. Through the land-grant university heritage, millions of students in each state and territory of the US are able to study every academic discipline and explore fields far beyond the scope envisioned in the original land-grant mission.

24. Which of the sentences below most clearly expresses important information in the highlighted sentences in paragraph 5? *Incorrect* choices change the meaning or leave out important information.

A Although land-grant colleges differ, schools of agriculture are more alike.

B Colleges of agriculture have a prominent place even today in college systems.

C Universities are mandated today to continue teaching agriculture.

D University expansion enabled colleges of agriculture to resemble one another.

25. **Directions:** Read the introductory sentence for a summary of the passage below. Complete the summary by choosing the THREE answer choices that include the key ideas in the passage. Some answer choices are incorrect because they include ideas that are not presented in the passage or are not significant in the passage. **This question is worth 2 points** (2 points for 3 correct answers, 1 point for 2 correct answers, and 0 points for 1 or 0 correct answers).

The passage discusses the American Land-Grant College System.

Fill in the oval next to your answer choice.

Choose three answers.

1 Most states used the grants to establish agricultural and mechanical arts colleges.

2 Many private colleges and universities became land-grant colleges.

3 The land-grant system helped extend higher education to working class families.

4 Land-grant colleges lost potential students to the Civil War.

5 Colleges of agriculture figure prominently in land-grant colleges today.

6 The system provided each state with 30,000 acres to establish a college or university.

Go on to the next page ➔

PART 2: READING 3

Read the passage.

Versatile Cotton

No one knows exactly how old cotton is. Scientists searching caves in Mexico found bits of cotton boils and pieces of cotton cloth that proved to be at least 7,000 years old. They also found the cotton itself was much like that grown in North America today. Archaeologists have discovered remnants of cotton cloth more than 4,000 years old along the Peruvian coast. Approximately 3,000 years ago cotton was being grown, spun, and woven into cloth in the Indus Valley in Pakistan. At about the same time, natives of Egypt's Nile Valley were making and wearing cotton clothing. Arab merchants brought cotton cloth to Europe about 800 A.D. When Columbus landed in America in 1492, he found cotton growing in the Bahamian Islands. By 1500 A.D., the plant had reached the warm regions of the Americas, Eurasia, and Africa and was known throughout the world.

Cotton was first spun by machinery in England in 1730. The industrial revolution in England coupled with the 1793 American invention of the cotton gin, short for engine, which could do the work ten times faster than by hand paved the way for the important place cotton holds in the world today. The gin made it possible to supply large quantities of cotton fiber to the fast-growing textile industry. Within ten years, the value of the US cotton crop rose from $150,000 to more than eight million dollars. In the 1850s a machine was invented to knock the hard hulls from the kernels of cottonseed, and so the cottonseed processing industry was born. In 1879 Ivory soap, made from the oil, was first produced. Around 1910 came America's first vegetable shortening, Crisco, which was made from cottonseed oil. Today, the world uses cottonseed oil in margarine, salad dressings, and cooking oils. Meal from the kernels is now made into fish bait, organic fertilizer and feed for cattle. In the coming years, new uses will probably continue to be discovered for this multi-purpose plant.

Currently, cotton is the best selling fiber throughout the world. Cotton comprises 61.5% of the total retail apparel and home furnishing market, aside from carpets, in the US. Most of the cotton that US mills spin and weave into cloth each year ends up as clothing. Cotton is frequently the fabric of choice as it absorbs color very well, and different textures can be achieved from different varieties of cotton. In addition to clothing, cotton is used in making such diverse items as book bindings, fish nets, handbags, coffee filters, lace, tents, curtains, and diapers.

Another attribute of cotton is its endurance. For this reason, it is an important component in medical supplies. Cotton is used for bandages and sutures because it will hold up in all kinds of environments. This durability also made it the preferred material for firefighting hoses. Fibers in the hoses would soak up water to prevent them from igniting. Today, however, fire hoses are usually made from synthetic materials that are cheaper and sturdier than cotton. In other environments, natural cotton is still the requested material for hoses; on US Navy ships the hoses are made of cotton because the sun tends to melt the synthetic, combustible materials. In addition, recent experiments have led scientists to think that cotton may be better for cleaning up oil spills than the synthetic material currently used.

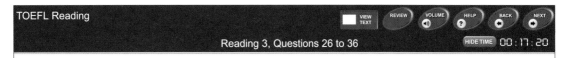

Companies have come up with innovative uses of cotton. Recycled old denim jeans could be used for durable housing insulation. With Americans buying 450 million pairs of jeans annually, weighing in at roughly 1 kilo or 2.2 pounds per pair, they are being looked at as a great source of high-quality material. Cotton is often criticized for its water-intense production, but with jeans living a second life as insulation, jeans could continue to be a stylish yet green lifestyle choice. An Alabama company is attempting to turn the by-product from cotton ginning into high quality mulch. While most other mulch, protective ground covering, is made from trees, this mulch is made using cotton gin trash. The result will reduce waste going to landfills, and mulch production will turn into a green industry itself. The all-natural mulch will reduce soil erosion on landscaping projects and should help grow healthy grass on lawns.

Refer to the passages below and answer the questions that follow.

Versatile Cotton

[1] No one knows exactly how old cotton is. Scientists searching caves in Mexico found bits of cotton boils and pieces of cotton cloth that proved to be at least 7,000 years old. They also found the cotton itself was much like that grown in North America today. Archaeologists have discovered remnants of cotton cloth more than 4,000 years old along the Peruvian coast. Approximately 3,000 years ago cotton was being grown, spun, and woven into cloth in the Indus Valley in Pakistan. At about the same time, natives of Egypt's Nile Valley were making and wearing cotton clothing. Arab merchants brought cotton cloth to Europe about 800 A.D. When Columbus landed in America in 1492, he found cotton growing in the Bahamian Islands. By 1500 A.D., the plant had reached the warm regions of the Americas, Eurasia, and Africa and was known throughout the world.

Directions: Fill in the oval next to your answer choice.

26. With which of the following is the passage primarily concerned?

    (A) The increasing number of uses of cotton

    (B) The history of the cotton textile industry

    (C) The development of the edible cottonseed

    (D) The shift of cotton from a textile crop to a food crop

[2] Cotton was first spun by machinery in England in 1730. The industrial revolution in England coupled with the 1793 American invention of the cotton gin, short for engine, which could do the work ten times faster than by hand paved the way for the important place cotton holds in the world today. The gin made it possible to supply large quantities of cotton fiber to the fast-growing textile industry. Within ten years, the value of the US cotton crop rose from $150,000 to more than eight million dollars. In the 1850s a machine was invented to knock the hard hulls from the kernels of cottonseed, and so the cottonseed processing industry was born. In 1879 Ivory soap, made from the oil, was first produced. Around 1910 came America's first vegetable shortening, Crisco, which was made from cottonseed oil. Today, the world uses cottonseed oil in margarine, salad dressings, and cooking oils. Meal from the kernels is now made into fish bait, organic fertilizer and feed for cattle. In the coming years, new uses will probably continue to be discovered for this multi-purpose plant.

27. How is paragraph 2 organized?

    (A) categorically

    (B) spatially

    (C) sequentially

    (D) chronologically

28. According to paragraph 2, the invention of the cotton gin was especially significant for which of the following reasons?

    (A) It contributed to the Industrial Revolution.

    (B) The textile industry was able to expand significantly.

    (C) It created the cottonseed processing industry.

    (D) Soaps and vegetable shortening resulted.

³ [29A] ■ Currently, cotton is the best selling fiber throughout the world. Cotton comprises 61.5% of the total retail apparel and home furnishing market, aside from carpets, in the US [29B] ■ Most of the cotton that US mills spin and weave into cloth each year ends up as clothing. [29C] ■ Cotton is frequently the fabric of choice as it absorbs color very well, and different textures can be achieved from different varieties of cotton. [29D] ■ In addition to clothing, cotton is used in making such diverse items as book bindings, fish nets, handbags, coffee filters, lace, tents, curtains, and diapers.

29. Look at the four squares [■] that show where the following sentence could be added to paragraph 3.

Cotton is a component of many items other than clothing.

Where would the sentence best fit?

    (A) [29A]

    (B) [29B]

    (C) [29C]

    (D) [29D]

⁴ Another attribute of cotton is its endurance. For this reason, it is an important component in medical supplies. Cotton is used for bandages and sutures because it will hold up in all kinds of environments. This durability also made it the preferred material for firefighting hoses. Fibers in the hoses would soak up water to prevent them from igniting. Today, however, fire hoses are usually made from synthetic materials that are cheaper and sturdier than cotton. In other environments, natural cotton is still the requested material for hoses; on US Navy ships the hoses are made of cotton because the sun tends to melt the synthetic, combustible materials. In addition, recent experiments have led scientists to think that cotton may be better for cleaning up oil spills than the synthetic material currently used.

30. The word "durability" in paragraph 4 is closest in meaning to

   (A) ignitability

   (B) preference

   (C) sturdiness

   (D) medication

31. The word "them" in paragraph 4 refers to

   (A) fibers

   (B) hoses

   (C) environments

   (D) kinds

32. Which of the sentences below most clearly expresses important information in the highlighted sentence in paragraph 4? *Incorrect* choices change the meaning or leave out important information.

   (A) The choice of artificial material for hoses is due to the cost and weakness of cotton.

   (B) Although cotton is a better product, fire hoses are made from synthetic material.

   (C) Cotton is no longer as durable as it once was.

   (D) Fire hose prices have increased due to the cost of cotton.

33. The word combustible in paragraph 4 is closest in meaning to

   (A) breakable

   (B) operational

   (C) flammable

   (D) artificial

⁵ Companies have come up with innovative uses of cotton. Recycled old denim jeans could be used for durable housing insulation. With Americans buying 450 million pairs of jeans annually, weighing in at roughly 1 kilo or 2.2 pounds per pair, they are being looked at as a great source of high-quality material. Cotton is often criticized for its water-intense production, but with jeans living a second life as insulation, jeans could continue to be a stylish yet green lifestyle choice. An Alabama company is attempting to turn the by-product from cotton ginning into high quality mulch. While most other mulch, protective ground covering, is made from trees, this mulch is made using cotton gin trash. The result will reduce waste going to landfills, and mulch production will turn into a green industry itself. The all-natural mulch will reduce soil erosion on landscaping projects and should help grow healthy grass on lawns.

34. The phrase "come up with" in paragraph 5 is closest in meaning to

   (A) sought

   (B) investigated

   (C) devised

   (D) attempted

Go on to the next page ➔

35. Match each description to the appropriate model on the right by placing a check mark (✓) in the correct boxes. **This question is worth 2 points** (2 points for 3 correct answers, 1 point for 2 correct answers, and 0 points for 1 or 0 correct answers).

	Organic fertilizer	Mulch	Housing insulation
By-product from cotton ginning			
Recycled old jeans			
Meal from cotton kernels			

36. **Directions:** The answer choices listed below each describe one of the uses of cotton today and possibly in the future. Complete the table by matching appropriate answer choices to the eras in which they were mentioned. Put a check mark in the correct boxes. TWO of the answer choices will NOT be used. This question is worth **4 points** (4 points for 7 correct answers, 3 points for 6 correct answers, 2 points for 5 correct answers, 1 point for 4 correct answers, and 0 points for 3, 2, 1, or 0 correct answers).

For each correct answer choice check the *Today* or *Future* column.

Choose seven answers.

	Today	Future
Housing insulation		
Medical supplies		
Soil erosion reduction		
Mulch		
Fire engines		
Navy ship fire hoses		
Cleaning oil spills		
Grass replacement		
Fish food		

Listening Section

This section tests your ability to understand conversations and lectures in English. You can listen to each conversation and lecture only **one** time.

After each conversation or lecture, you will answer some questions. The questions usually ask about the main idea and supporting details or about a speaker's attitude or purpose. Answer the questions based on what the speakers say or imply.

You can take notes while you listen. The notes may help you answer the questions. You will NOT receive a score for your notes.

You will see the **audio icon** 🎧 in some questions. This means that you will hear a part of the question that does not appear on the test page.

Questions are worth 1 point. If a question is worth more than 1 point, specific directions will tell you how many points you can receive.

You will have **60 minutes** to listen to the conversations and lectures and to answer the questions. You should answer each question even if your answer is only a guess.

PART 1

Questions 1–5

🎧 Listen to Track 20.

Listen as a student consults with a professor.

NOTES:

Directions: Fill in the oval next to your answer choice.

1. Why does the student go to see the professor?

   Ⓐ To get a recommendation for medical school

   Ⓑ To ask about changing advisors

   Ⓒ To find out how many required courses she has

   Ⓓ To consult about switching majors

2. What is stated about science prerequisites?

   Choose 2 answers.

   Ⓐ The student thinks they are more difficult than other subjects.

   Ⓑ She has seven or eight left to take.

   Ⓒ If she takes them, they will bring up her GPA.

   Ⓓ She has already taken many of them.

3. What incorrect assumption did the professor make?

   Ⓐ That premed courses are offered every semester

   Ⓑ That medical schools prefer science major applicants

   Ⓒ That the student had a different advisor

   Ⓓ That she wouldn't be able to complete all the coursework

4. What did the student say medical schools consider?

   Choose 3 answers.

   Ⓐ A student's GPA

   Ⓑ The entrance exam score

   Ⓒ Recommendations

   Ⓓ Having taken the prereqs

   Ⓔ Personal interview

5. What does the student say about the "What If?" link?

   Ⓐ She is not sure the professor knows about it.

   Ⓑ It told her how many courses she needs if she switches majors

   Ⓒ She can use it in place of conferring with an advisor

   Ⓓ It is a new program for business and history majors

Questions 6–10

🎧 Listen to Track 21.

Listen to a discussion in a fashion design class.

NOTES:

Directions: Fill in the oval next to your answer choice.

6. What are the students and professor mainly discussing?

    (A) How flip-flops became mainstream footwear

    (B) Flip-flop design

    (C) Flip-flops and medical problems

    (D) The evolution of flip-flops

7. According to the professor, what are other names for flip-flops around the world?

    Choose 3 answers.

    (A) Y-shaped straps

    (B) Zori

    (C) Jandals

    (D) Thongs

    (E) Beach shoes

8. Match each sandal material in the box below to its location by placing a check mark (✓) in the correct box. **This question is worth 2 points** (2 points for 3 correct answers, 1 point for 2 correct answers, and 0 points for 1 or 0 correct answers).

Each answer will be used one time only. Only three answers are correct.

	Masai of Africa	India	Europe
Papyrus leaves			
Rawhide			
Rice straw			
Wood			
Yucca plant			

9. Play Track 22 to listen again to part of the lecture. Then answer the question.

Why does the professor say this?

    (A) Because it is a very warm day

    (B) Because flip-flops are typically water shoes

    (C) Because the discussion is going to be about flip-flops

    (D) Because she is not wearing them

10. What does the professor say are likely causes for foot problems from wearing flip-flops?

    Choose 2 answers.

    (A) Thick-cushioned soles

    (B) Lack of support

    (C) Scrunching toes

    (D) Y-shaped straps

Go on to the next page ➔

Questions 11–16

🎧 Listen to Track 23.

expert witness

NOTES:

Directions: Fill in the oval next to your answer choice.

11. What does the lecturer mainly discuss?

   (A) The role of the expert witness in court cases

   (B) Why expert witnesses must take the stand

   (C) The expense involved in hiring expert witnesses

   (D) What to consider when choosing an expert witness

12. Why does the professor mention that an expert witness must be someone the jury will understand?

   (A) Because expert witnesses do not usually talk with jurors

   (B) Because jurors may not understand the language of experts

   (C) Because expert witnesses need to be familiar with the jurors

   (D) Because jurors need to get along with expert witnesses

13. What does the professor NOT say about using doctors as expert witnesses?

   (A) The more impressive the credentials, the better.

   (B) They must be working.

   (C) It's preferable that they have published.

   (D) They must have a state license.

14. What does the lecturer say can be a problem of using a professional witness?

   (A) They may not have written anything.

   (B) They can be expensive to hire.

   (C) They may not understand the pressure in a cross-examination.

   (D) It is better to hire one who has not published.

🎧 15. Play Track 24 to listen again to part of the lecture. Then answer the question. Why does the professor say this?

   (A) Because he thinks the students can identify with juror reactions.

   (B) Because he expects that the students will be on a jury one day.

   (C) Because he is trying to stop the lecture for a minute

   (D) Because he wants them to imagine being an expert witness

16. What is stated in the lecture about being an expert witness?

   Choose 2 answers.

   (A) There are specific requirements that all witnesses must meet.

   (B) It is a problem if the witness has written something that contradicts the testimony.

   (C) The expert witness will charge twice as much as a normal hourly wage.

   (D) Depending on the type of trial, a witness need not have advanced degrees.

Go on to the next page ➜

PART 2

Questions 17–22

🎧 Listen to Track 25.

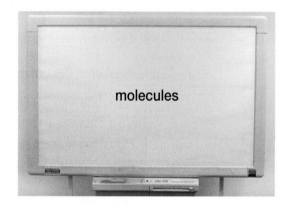

NOTES:

Directions: Listen to part of a lecture in a chemistry class.

17. What does the professor mainly discuss?

    (A) The syllabus of the inorganic chemistry course

    (B) How inorganic chemistry differs from organic chemistry

    (C) The basic chemical structure of organic molecules

    (D) The substances taken for granted

18. According to the discussion, what questions can be answered by examining molecules?

    Choose 2 answers.

    (A) Why garlic smells

    (B) What pills are made of

    (C) Why we fill up our cars

    (D) Why we need to exercise

19. What is NOT stated in the lecture about inorganic chemistry?

    (A) Organic molecules constitute the building blocks of life.

    (B) Organic chemistry studies carbon and its compounds.

    (C) Molecules are made up of chemicals that regulate our bodies.

    (D) There are different molecular compositions in the clothes we wear.

20. What does the professor say is the principal component of fats, sugars, and the nucleic acid compounds?

    (A) organic substances

    (B) natural fibers

    (C) carbon

    (D) proteins

21. Play Track 26 to listen again to part of the passage. Then answer the question. Why does the professor say this?

    (A) He is presenting a specific example.

    (B) He cannot remember any examples.

    (C) He wants the students to name the industries.

    (D) He is injecting a bit of humor into the discussion.

22. Which organic substance does the professor NOT mention as one that has improved the quality of life?

    (A) gasoline

    (B) medicine

    (C) fats and sugars

    (D) pesticides

Go on to the next page ➔

Questions 23–28

🎧 Listen to Track 27.

NOTES:

Directions: Listen to a lecture in a dental hygiene class.

23. What main point does the professor make about chewing gum?

    (A) More than 50 million hours of school are missed every year because of gum.

    (B) Children should chew xylitol gum in moderation.

    (C) Chewing xylitol gum increases saliva production.

    (D) Teeth can handle some gum chewing exposure to acids.

24. Play Track 28 to listen again to part of the passage. Then answer the question. Why does the professor say this?

    (A) To contrast with what happens in classrooms

    (B) To tell what she had to do when she was in school

    (C) To explain a reason why gum chewing was unacceptable

    (D) To let the students know they will have to clean their desks

25. In the talk, the professor describes the stages in cavity formulation. Summarize the sequence by putting the stages in the correct order. Number each stage 1, 2, 3, or 4.

This question is worth 2 points (2 points for 3 correct answers, 1 point for 2 correct answers, and 0 points for 1 or 0 correct answers).

_____ Demineralization occurs.

_____ Saliva is overwhelmed.

_____ Acids are produced.

_____ Bacteria encounter sugar.

26. What does the professor say about chewing gum?

Choose 3 answers.

    (A) Chewing gum of any kind increases saliva production.

    (B) Chewing sugar produces acids.

    (C) Chewing xylitol sweetened gum inhibits bacteria growth.

    (D) Chewing xylitol sweetened gum increases the acid level.

    (E) Chewing xylitol sweetened gum decreases saliva production.

27. According to the lecturer, why have school administrators NOT implemented gum chewing?

    (A) They do not want children to have ear infections.

    (B) They do not like children to blow bubbles in class.

    (C) They may not know about the international data.

    (D) They do now want to clean gum off of desks.

28. What does the professor suggest the optimal gum chewing regimen be?

    (A) 3 times daily, 3 to 5 minutes each time

    (B) 3 to 5 times daily, 3 minutes each time

    (C) 3 to 5 times daily, 5 minutes each time

    (D) 5 times daily, 3 to 5 minutes each time

Go on to the next page ➜

Questions 29–34

🎧 Listen to Track 29.

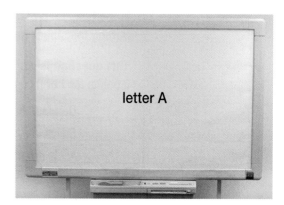

NOTES:

Directions: Listen to a lecture in a linguistics class.

29. What is the main topic of the lecture?

  (A) The Phoenician dominance in spreading the alphabet

  (B) The history and transformation of the letter A

  (C) Why some celebrities are called A-list ones

  (D) How the formation of the letter A has changed

30. What is true about the original alphabet?

  Choose 2 answers.

  (A) It was developed by the Phoenicians.

  (B) The Hebrews created their own symbols.

  (C) Semitic people living in or near Egypt developed it.

  (D) It was quickly adopted by neighbors.

31. Why does the professor mention the aleph pictogram?

  (A) To connect the Phoenician and Egyptian alphabets

  (B) To contrast subsequent aleph forms

  (C) To explain the importance of oxen in Egyptian life

  (D) To suggest the basis of the aleph design

32. Which of the following are true about the lower case letter A?

  Choose 2 answers.

  (A) The forms used in print and handwriting are different.

  (B) The printed form and the handwritten form are the same.

  (C) Both forms of lower case A derive from the capital letter form.

  (D) The form used in handwriting resembles the Hebrew letter aleph.

33. Who brought the Greek alphabet to their civilization in the Italian peninsula?

  (A) The Spaniards

  (B) The Phoenicians

  (C) The Romans

  (D) The Etruscans

34. What is true about the English letter A?

  Choose 2 answers.

  (A) In English the letter A has four different vowel sounds.

  (B) The most common A sounds are "ay" in "day" and "eh" in "mad."

  (C) The letter A is the second most common letter used in English.

  (D) An A is often used to signify the best performance.

STOP. This is the end of the Listening section.

Speaking

This section tests your ability to speak about different topics. You will answer six questions.

Questions 1 and 2 will be about familiar topics.

Questions 3 and 4 will include reading and listening passages. First, you will read a short passage. Then you will hear a talk about the same topic. Next you will answer a question about the text and the talk. Use the information from the text and the talk to show that you understood both of them.

Questions 5 and 6 will include part of a conversation or a lecture and a question. Use the information from the conversation and the lecture to show that you understood both of them.

While you read and listen, you can take notes that should help you answer the questions.

Listen carefully to the directions for each question. The preparation time begins right after you hear the question. You will be told when to begin to prepare and when to begin speaking.

QUESTIONS

Track 30

1. You will hear a question about a familiar topic. Listen to the question, and then prepare a response. You will have 15 seconds to prepare a response and 45 seconds to speak. You can take notes on the main points of a response.

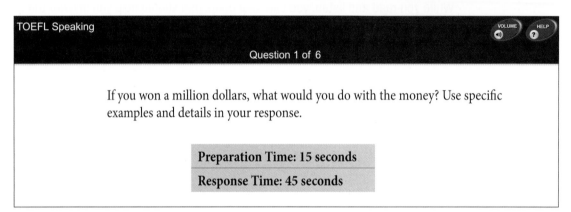

TOEFL Speaking

VOLUME   HELP

Question 1 of 6

If you won a million dollars, what would you do with the money? Use specific examples and details in your response.

Preparation Time: 15 seconds

Response Time: 45 seconds

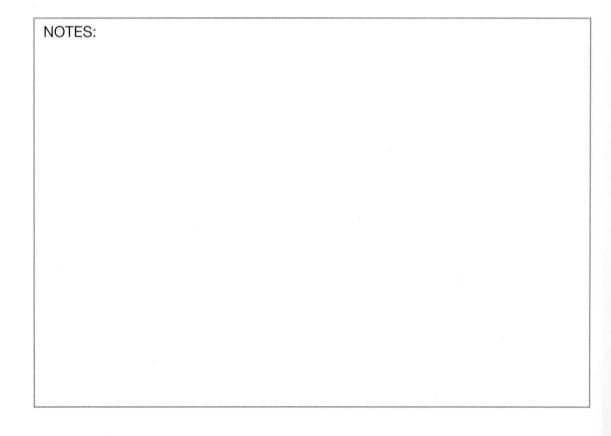

NOTES:

Track 31

2. You will be asked your opinion about a familiar topic. Listen to the question, and then prepare your response. You will have 15 seconds to prepare a response and 45 seconds to speak. You can take notes on the main points of a response.

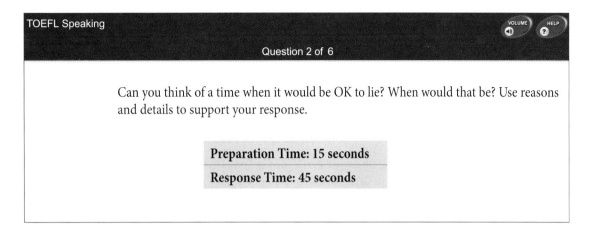

NOTES:

Track 32

3. You will read a short passage and then listen to a conversation about the same topic. You will then answer a question about about them. You will have 45 seconds to read the passage. You can take notes on the main points of the reading passage.

Reading Time: 45 seconds

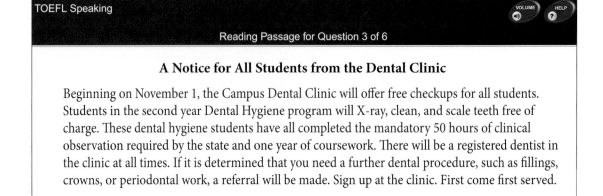

TOEFL Speaking

VOLUME   HELP

Reading Passage for Question 3 of 6

A Notice for All Students from the Dental Clinic

Beginning on November 1, the Campus Dental Clinic will offer free checkups for all students. Students in the second year Dental Hygiene program will X-ray, clean, and scale teeth free of charge. These dental hygiene students have all completed the mandatory 50 hours of clinical observation required by the state and one year of coursework. There will be a registered dentist in the clinic at all times. If it is determined that you need a further dental procedure, such as fillings, crowns, or periodontal work, a referral will be made. Sign up at the clinic. First come first served.

Listen to the conversation. You can take notes on the main points of the conversation.

NOTES:

Now answer the following question:

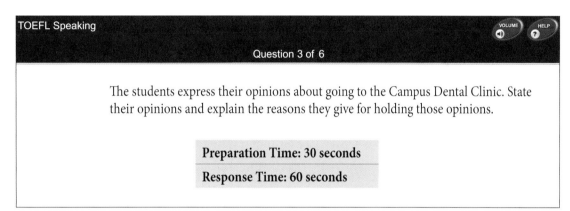

The students express their opinions about going to the Campus Dental Clinic. State their opinions and explain the reasons they give for holding those opinions.

Preparation Time: 30 seconds
Response Time: 60 seconds

NOTES:

Track 33

4. You will read a short passage and then listen to a conversation about the same topic. You will then answer a question about about them. You will have 45 seconds to read the passage. You can take notes on the main points of the reading passage.

Reading Time: 45 seconds

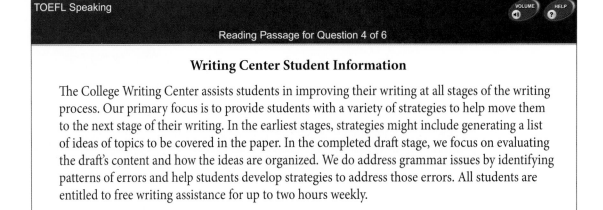

TOEFL Speaking

VOLUME   HELP

Reading Passage for Question 4 of 6

Writing Center Student Information

The College Writing Center assists students in improving their writing at all stages of the writing process. Our primary focus is to provide students with a variety of strategies to help move them to the next stage of their writing. In the earliest stages, strategies might include generating a list of ideas of topics to be covered in the paper. In the completed draft stage, we focus on evaluating the draft's content and how the ideas are organized. We do address grammar issues by identifying patterns of errors and help students develop strategies to address those errors. All students are entitled to free writing assistance for up to two hours weekly.

Listen to the passage. You can take notes on the main points of the listening passage.

NOTES:

Now answer the following question:

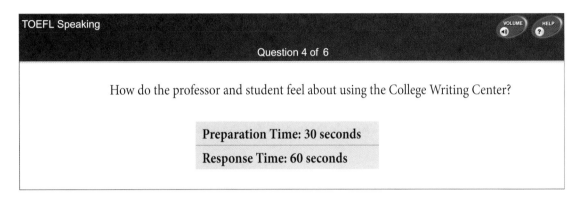

How do the professor and student feel about using the College Writing Center?

Preparation Time: 30 seconds

Response Time: 60 seconds

Track 34

5. You will listen to part of a lecture. You can take notes on the main points of the listening passage.

Now answer the following question:

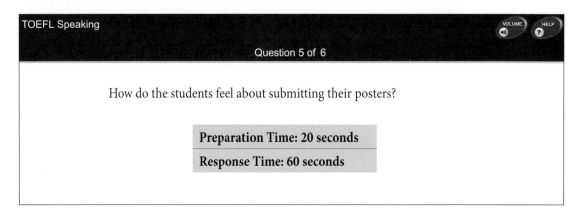

How do the students feel about submitting their posters?

Preparation Time: 20 seconds

Response Time: 60 seconds

NOTES:

Go on to the next page ➔

Track 35

6. Listen to part of a lecture. You can take notes on the main points of the listening passage.

Now answer the following question:

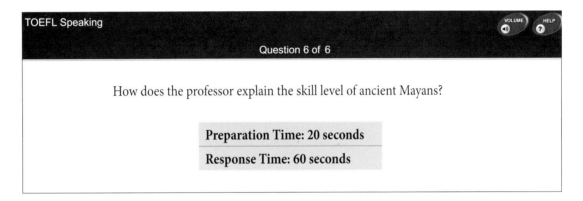

NOTES:

STOP. This is the end of the Speaking section.

Writing Section

This section tests your ability to use writing in an academic setting. There will be two writing tasks.

In the first writing task, the integrated writing task, you will read a passage and listen to a lecture. You will then answer a question based on the reading passage and the lecture. In the second task, the independent writing task, you will answer a question using your own background knowledge.

Integrated Writing Directions

For this task, you will read a passage about an academic topic, and then you will hear a lecture about the same topic. You can take notes on both.

Then you will read a question about the connection between the reading passage and the lecture. In your written response try to use information from both the passage and the lecture. You will **not** be asked for your own opinion. You can refer the reading passage while you are writing.

You should plan on **3 minutes** to read the passage. Then listen to the lecture and give yourself **20 minutes** to plan and write your response. A successful response will be about 150 to 225 words. Your response will be judged on the quality of the writing and the correctness of the content.

QUESTION 1

Read the passage. On a piece of paper, take notes on the main points of the reading passage.

> **Reading Time: 3 minutes**

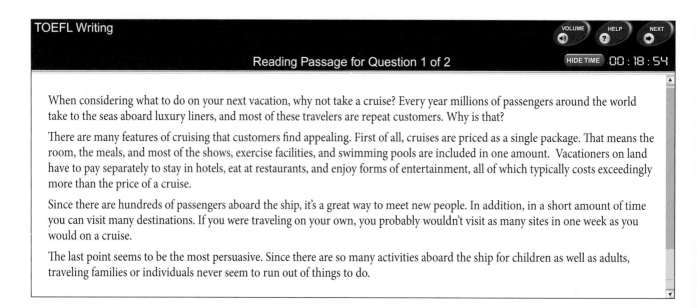

TOEFL Writing

Reading Passage for Question 1 of 2

VOLUME   HELP   NEXT

HIDE TIME   00 : 18 : 54

When considering what to do on your next vacation, why not take a cruise? Every year millions of passengers around the world take to the seas aboard luxury liners, and most of these travelers are repeat customers. Why is that?

There are many features of cruising that customers find appealing. First of all, cruises are priced as a single package. That means the room, the meals, and most of the shows, exercise facilities, and swimming pools are included in one amount. Vacationers on land have to pay separately to stay in hotels, eat at restaurants, and enjoy forms of entertainment, all of which typically costs exceedingly more than the price of a cruise.

Since there are hundreds of passengers aboard the ship, it's a great way to meet new people. In addition, in a short amount of time you can visit many destinations. If you were traveling on your own, you probably wouldn't visit as many sites in one week as you would on a cruise.

The last point seems to be the most persuasive. Since there are so many activities aboard the ship for children as well as adults, traveling families or individuals never seem to run out of things to do.

🎧 Play Track 36 to listen to the passage.

Now answer the following question:

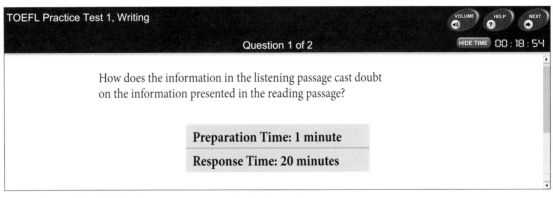

Write your response here or on a computer.

_____

_____

_____

_____

_____

_____

_____

_____

Go on to the next page →

Independent Writing Directions

For this task, you will write an essay that explains, supports, and states your opinion about an issue. You will have **30 minutes** to plan, write, and edit your essay. You can take notes on the main points of a response.

A successful response will be at least 300 words. Try to show that you can develop your ideas, organize your essay, and use language correctly to express your ideas. The essay will be judged on the quality of your writing.

QUESTION 2

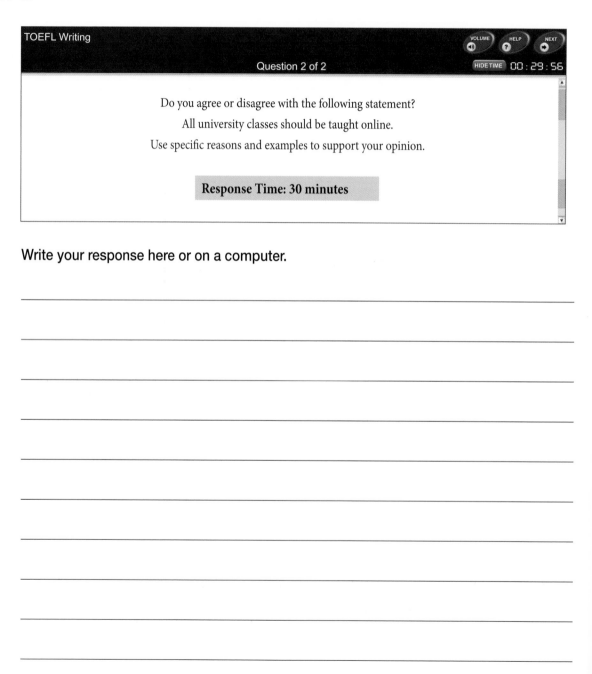

Do you agree or disagree with the following statement?

All university classes should be taught online.

Use specific reasons and examples to support your opinion.

Response Time: 30 minutes

Write your response here or on a computer.

Go on to the next page →

STOP. This is the end of the Writing section.

Mini-Dictionary

abstract /ˈæbstrækt/ (abstracts)

ADJECTIVE An **abstract** idea or way of thinking is based on general ideas rather than on real things and events. ○ *abstract principles such as justice* ○ *Fractional dimension is an abstract concept that enables mathematicians to measure the complexity of an object.* ○ *the faculty of abstract reasoning*

adhere /ædˈhɪər/ (adheres, adhering, adhered)

VERB If you **adhere to** a rule or agreement, you act in the way that it says you should. ○ *All members of the association adhere to a strict code of practice.*

affect /əˈfɛkt/ (affects, affecting, affected)

VERB If something **affects** a person or thing, it influences them or causes them to change in some way. ○ *Price changes must not adversely affect the living standards of the people.* ○ *More than seven million people have been affected by drought.* ○ *The new law will directly affect thousands of people.* ○ *Noise in factories can seriously affect workers' health.*

annually /ˈænyuəli/

ADVERB If an event takes place **annually**, it happens once every year. ○ *Production costs are reviewed annually to ensure the company is not wasting money.*

apprentice /əˈprɛntɪs/ apprentices

NOUN An **apprentice** is a young person who works for someone in order to learn their skill. ○ *I started off as an apprentice and worked my way up.*

aspect /ˈæspɛkt/ aspects

NOUN An **aspect** of something is one of the parts of its character or nature. ○ *Climate and weather affect every aspect of our lives.* ○ *a framework covering different aspects of telecommunications and information technology*

assert /əˈsɜrt/ (asserts, asserting, asserted)

VERB If someone **asserts** a fact or belief, they state it firmly. [FORMAL] ○ *Mr. Helm plans to assert that the bill violates the First Amendment.* ○ *The defendants, who continue to assert their innocence, are expected to appeal.* ○ *Altman asserted, "We were making a political statement about western civilization and greed."* ○ *The American sugar industry has repeatedly asserted that quotas ensure a reliable supply of sugar.*

assume /əˈsum/ (assumes, assuming, assumed)

VERB If you **assume that** something is true, you imagine that it is true, sometimes wrongly. ○ *It is a misconception to assume that the two continents are similar.* ○ *If mistakes occurred, they were assumed to be the fault of the commander on the spot.*

astounding /əˈstaʊndɪŋ/

ADJECTIVE If something is **astounding**, you are shocked or amazed that it could exist or happen. ○ *The results are quite astounding.*

astute /əˈstut/

ADJECTIVE If you describe someone as **astute**, you think they show an understanding of behavior and situations, and are skillful at using this knowledge to their own advantage. ○ *She was politically astute.*

background /ˈbækɡraʊnd/ (backgrounds)

NOUN The **background to** an event or situation consists of the facts that explain what caused it. ○ *The meeting takes place against a background of continuing political violence.* ○ *The background to the experience is important.*

basis /ˈbeɪsɪs/ (bases)

NOUN The **basis** of something is its starting point or an important part of it from which it can be further developed. ○ *Both factions have broadly agreed that the U.N. plan is a possible basis for negotiation.*

building block /ˈbɪldɪŋ blɒk/ (building blocks)

NOUN If you describe something as a **building block** of something, you mean it is one of the separate parts that combine to make that thing. ○ *molecules that are the building blocks of all life on earth*

capital /ˈkæpɪtəl/ (capitals)

NOUN **Capitals** or **capital letters** are written or printed letters in the form which is used at the beginning of sentences or names. "T," "B," and "F" are capitals. ○ *The name and address are written in capitals.*

characteristic /ˌkærɪktəˈrɪstɪk/ (characteristics)

NOUN The **characteristics** of a person or thing are the qualities or features that belong to them and make them recognizable. ○ *Genes determine the characteristics of every living thing.* ○ *their physical characteristics*

circulate /ˈsɜrkyəleɪt/ (circulates, circulating, circulated)

VERB When something **circulates**, it moves easily and freely within a closed place or system. ○ *a virus which circulates via the bloodstream* ○ *the sound of water circulating through pipes*

clarify /ˈklærɪfaɪ/ (clarifies, clarifying, clarified)

VERB To **clarify** something means to make it easier to understand, usually by explaining it in more detail. [FORMAL] ○ *It is important to clarify the distinction between the relativity of values and the relativity of truth.* ○ *A bank spokesman was unable to clarify the situation.* ○ *You will want to clarify what your objectives are.*

classical studies /ˈklæsɪkəl ˈstʌdiz/

NONCOUNT NOUN **Classical studies** is the study of ancient Greek or Roman civilizations, especially their languages, literature, and philosophy. ○ *a classical studies degree* ○ *He was a classical studies major, and he could read Latin as if it were English.*

clinical /klɪnɪkəl/

ADJECTIVE **Clinical** means involving or relating to the direct medical treatment or testing of patients. ○ *The first clinical trials were expected to begin next year.* ○ *a clinical psychologist* ○ *the clinical aftereffects of the accident*

colonist /kɒlənɪst/ (**colonists**)

NOUN **Colonists** are the people who start a colony or the people who are among the first to live in a particular colony. ○ *The apple was brought over here by the colonists when they came.*

combustible /kəmbʌstɪbəl/

ADJECTIVE A **combustible** material or gas catches fire and burns easily. [FORMAL] ○ *The ability of coal to release a combustible gas has long been known.*

come up with (**comes, coming, came**)

PHRASAL VERB If you **come up with** an idea or solution, you find it or propose it. ○ *Several of the members have come up with suggestions of their own.*

component /kəmpoʊnənt/ (**components**)

NOUN The **components** of something are the parts that it is made of. ○ *Enriched uranium is a key component of a nuclear weapon.* ○ *The management plan has four main components.* ○ *The companies concerned were automotive component suppliers to the car manufacturers.*

comprise /kəmpraɪz/ (**comprises, comprising, comprised**)

VERB If you say that something **comprises** or **is comprised of** a number of things or people, you mean it has them as its parts or members. [FORMAL] ○ *The exhibition comprises 50 oils and watercolors.* ○ *The Coordinating Group is currently comprised of representatives from 73 financial institutions.*

consist /kənsɪst/ (**consists, consisting, consisted**)

VERB Something that **consists of** particular things or people is formed from them. ○ *Breakfast consisted of toast served with butter.* ○ *Her crew consisted of children from Maine and New Hampshire.*

constantly /kɒnstəntli/

ADVERB If something happens **constantly**, or if you do something **constantly**, it happens all the time. ○ *The direction of the wind is constantly changing.*

contemplate /kɒntəmpleɪt/ (**contemplates, contemplating, contemplated**)

VERB If you **contemplate** an action, you think about whether to do it or not. ○ *For a time, he contemplated a career as a medical doctor in the army.*

contribution /kɒntrɪbyuʃən/ (**contributions**)

NOUN If you make a **contribution to** something, you do something to help make it successful or to produce it. ○ *American economists have made important contributions to the field of financial and corporate economics.* ○ *He was awarded a prize for his contribution to world peace.*

course /kɔrs/ (**courses**)

NOUN A **course** is a series of lessons or lectures on a particular subject. ○ *universities that offer courses in business administration* ○ *a course on the modern novel*

criterion /kraɪtɪəriən/ (**criteria**)

NOUN A **criterion** is a factor on which you judge or decide something. ○ *The most important criterion for entry is that applicants must design and make their own work.* ○ *Our defense policy had to meet three criteria if it was to succeed.*

crop /krɒp/ (**crops**)

NOUN **Crops** are plants such as wheat and potatoes that are grown in large quantities, usually for food. ○ *Rice farmers here still plant and harvest their crops by hand.* ○ *The main crop is wheat, and this is grown even on the very steep slopes.*

cubbyhole /kʌbi hoʊl/ (**cubbyholes**)

NOUN A **cubbyhole** is a very small room or space for storing things. ○ *It's in the cubbyhole under the stairs.*

cultivated /kʌltɪveɪtɪd/

ADJECTIVE If you describe someone as **cultivated**, you mean they are well educated and have good manners. [FORMAL] ○ *His mother was an elegant, cultivated woman.*

curb /kɜrb/ (**curbs**)

NOUN The **curb** is the raised edge of a sidewalk which separates it from the road. ○ *I pulled over to the curb.*

deadline /dɛdlaɪn/ (**deadlines**)

NOUN A **deadline** is a time or date before which a particular task must be finished or a particular thing must be done. ○ *We were not able to meet the deadline because of manufacturing delays.*

debunk /dibʌŋk/ (**debunks, debunking, debunked**)

VERB If you **debunk** a widely held belief, you show that it is false. If you **debunk** something that is widely admired, you show that it is not as good as people think it is. ○ *Historian Michael Beschloss debunks a few myths.*

decimate /dɛsɪmeɪt/ (**decimates, decimating, decimated**)

VERB To **decimate** something such as a group of people or animals means to destroy a very large number of them. ○ *The pollution could decimate the river's thriving population of kingfishers.*

declare /dɪklɛər/ (**declares, declaring, declared**)

VERB If you **declare** something, you state officially and formally that it exists or is the case. ○ *The government is ready to declare a permanent ceasefire.* ○ *His lawyers are confident that the judges will declare Mr. Stevens innocent.* ○ *The U.N. has declared it to be a safe zone.*

decline /dɪklaɪn/ (**declines**)

NOUN If there is a **decline in** something, it becomes less in quantity, importance, or quality. ○ *The reasons for the apparent decline in fertility are unclear.* ○ *Rome's decline in the fifth century* ○ *The first signs of economic decline became visible.*

detect /dɪtɛkt/ **(detects, detecting, detected)**
VERB To **detect** something means to find it or discover that it is present somewhere by using equipment or making an investigation. ○ *a sensitive piece of equipment used to detect radiation* ○ *Most skin cancers can be cured if detected and treated early.*

determine /dɪtɜrmɪn/ **(determines, determining, determined)**
VERB To **determine** a fact means to discover it as a result of investigation. [FORMAL] ○ *The investigation will determine what actually happened.* ○ *Testing needs to be done to determine the long-term effects on humans.* ○ *Science has determined that the risk is very small.*

device /dɪvaɪs/ **(devices)**
NOUN A **device** is an object that has been invented for a particular purpose, for example, for recording or measuring something. ○ *an electronic device that protects your vehicle 24 hours a day* ○ *An explosive device had been left inside a container.*

digit /dɪdʒɪt/ **(digits)**
NOUN A **digit** is a written symbol for any of the ten numbers from 0 to 9. ○ *Her telephone number differs from mine by one digit.* ○ *Inflation is still in double digits.*

dilemma (dɪlɛmə) **(dilemmas)**
NOUN A **dilemma** is a difficult situation in which you have to choose between two or more alternatives. ○ *He was faced with the dilemma of whether or not to return to his country.* ○ *The issue raises a moral dilemma.*

display /dɪspleɪ/ **(displays, displaying, displayed)**
VERB When a computer **displays** information, it shows it on a screen. ○ *They started out by looking at the computer screens which display the images.*

disposal /dɪspoʊzəl/
NONCOUNT NOUN **Disposal** is the act of getting rid of something that is no longer wanted or needed. ○ *methods for the permanent disposal of radioactive waste*

disprove /dɪspruv/ **(disproves, disproving, disproved, disproven)**
VERB To **disprove** an idea, belief, or theory means to show that it is not true. ○ *The statistics to prove or disprove his hypothesis will take years to collect.* ○ *articles claiming to disprove the global-warming theory*

distinguished /dɪstɪŋgwɪʃt/
ADJECTIVE If you describe a person, an organization, or their work as **distinguished**, you mean that they have been very successful and have a good reputation. ○ *a distinguished academic family*

diverse /dɪvɜrs/
ADJECTIVE **Diverse** people or things are very different from each other. ○ *Albert Jones's new style will put him in touch with a much more diverse and perhaps younger audience.*

doggedly /dɒgɪdli/
ADVERB If you say that someone does something **doggedly**, you mean that they are determined to continue with it even if it becomes difficult or dangerous. ○ *She would fight doggedly for her rights as the children's mother.*

domestic /dəmɛstɪk/
ADJECTIVE **Domestic** means relating to or concerned with the home and family. ○ *a plan for sharing domestic chores* ○ *the sale of furniture and domestic appliances* ○ *victims of domestic violence*

dominant /dɒmɪnənt/
ADJECTIVE Someone or something that is **dominant** is more powerful, successful, influential, or noticeable than other people or things. ○ *a change that would maintain his party's dominant position in Texas* ○ *She was a dominant figure in the French film industry.*

draft /dræft/ **(drafts)**
NOUN A **draft** is an early version of a piece of writing. ○ *a draft report from a major U.S. university* ○ *a final draft of an essay*

durability /dʊərəbɪlɪti/
NONCOUNT NOUN **Durability** is the quality of being strong and being able to last a long time without breaking or becoming weaker. ○ *Airlines recommend hard-sided cases for durability.*

earth-shattering /ɜrθʃætərɪŋ/
ADJECTIVE Something that is **earth-shattering** is very surprising or shocking. ○ *a truly earth-shattering discovery*

effect /ɪfɛkt/ **(effects)**
NOUN The **effect of** one thing **on** another is the change that the first thing causes in the second thing. ○ *The Internet could have a significant effect on trade in the next few years.* ○ *The housing market is feeling the effects of the increase in interest rates.* ○ *Even minor head injuries can cause long-lasting psychological effects.*

element /ɛlɪmənt/ **(elements)**
NOUN The different **elements** of a situation, activity, or process are the different parts of it. ○ *The exchange of prisoners of war was one of the key elements of the U.N.'s peace plan.* ○ *The plot has all the elements not only of romance but of high drama.*

emit /ɪmɪt/ **(emits, emitting, emitted)**
VERB If something **emits** heat, light, gas, or a smell, it produces it and sends it out by means of a physical or chemical process. [FORMAL] ○ *The new device emits a powerful circular column of light.* ○ *the amount of carbon dioxide emitted*

enact /ɪnækt/ **(enacts, enacting, enacted)**
VERB If a particular event or situation **is enacted**, it happens; used especially to talk about something that has happened before. ○ *We could sense something of the tragedy that was being enacted in Europe.*

enactment /ɪnˈæktmənt/ **(enactments)**

NOUN The **enactment of** a law is the process in a legislature by which the law is agreed upon and made official. ○ *We support the call for the enactment of a Bill of Rights.*

encompass /ɪnˈkʌmpəs/ **(encompasses, encompassing, encompassed)**

VERB If something **encompasses** particular things, it includes them. ○ *His repertoire encompassed everything from Bach to Schoenberg.*

endow /ɪnˈdaʊ/ **(endows, endowing, endowed)**

VERB If someone **endows** an institution, scholarship, or project, they provide a large amount of money that will produce the income needed to pay for it. ○ *The ambassador has endowed a $1 million public-service fellowships program.*

endure /ɪnˈdʊər/ **(endures, enduring, endured)**

VERB If something or someone **endures** a force or action, they survive it or do not give in to it. ○ *He did not have to endure the numbing effect of an English February.* ○ *He endured a lot of suffering during his life.*

ensure /ɪnˈʃʊər/ **(ensures, ensuring, ensured)**

VERB To **ensure** something, or to **ensure that** something happens, means to make certain that it happens. [FORMAL] ○ *The United States' negotiators had ensured that the treaty was a significant change in direction.* ○ *Ensure that it is written into your contract.*

era /ˈɪərə/ **(eras)**

NOUN You can refer to a period of history or a long period of time as an **era** when you want to draw attention to a particular feature or quality that it has. ○ *the nuclear era* ○ *It was an era of austerity.*

evidence /ˈɛvɪdəns/

NONCOUNT NOUN **Evidence** is anything that you see, experience, read, or are told that causes you to believe that something is true or has really happened. ○ *The results gave clear statistical evidence of these phenomena.* ○ *Ganley said he'd seen no evidence of widespread fraud.*

evolution /ˌivəˈluʃ°n, ˌɛv-/

NONCOUNT NOUN **Evolution** is a process of gradual development in a particular situation or thing over a period of time. ○ *a crucial period in the evolution of modern physics*

exclude /ɪksˈkluːd/ **(excludes, excluding, excluded)**

VERB If you **exclude** something that has some connection with what you are doing, you deliberately do not use it or consider it. ○ *They eat only plant food and take care to exclude animal products from other areas of their lives.*

exhibit /ɪgˈzɪbɪt/ **(exhibits)**

NOUN An **exhibit** is a painting, sculpture, or object of interest that is displayed to the public in a museum or art gallery. ○ *Shona showed me around the exhibits.*

expenditure /ɪksˈpɛndɪtʃər/

NONCOUNT NOUN **Expenditure** is the spending of money on something, or the money that is spent on something. [FORMAL] ○ *Policies of tax reduction must lead to reduced public expenditure.* ○ *They should cut their expenditure on defense.*

expertise /ˌɛkspɜrˈtiz/

NONCOUNT NOUN **Expertise** is special skill or knowledge that is acquired by training, study, or practice. ○ *Most local authorities lack the expertise to deal sensibly in this market.* ○ *students with expertise in forensics* ○ *a pooling and sharing of knowledge and expertise*

exploit /ɪksˈplɔɪt/ **(exploits, exploiting, exploited)**

VERB If you **exploit** something, you use it well, and achieve something or gain an advantage from it. ○ *Cary is hoping to exploit new opportunities in Europe.* ○ *So you feel that your skills have never been fully appreciated or exploited?*

field /ˈfild/ **(fields)**

NOUN A particular **field** is a particular subject of study or type of activity. ○ *Exciting artistic breakthroughs have recently occurred in the fields of painting, sculpture, and architecture.* ○ *Each of the authors is an expert in his field.*

found /ˈfaʊnd/ **(founds, founding, founded)**

VERB When an institution, company, or organization **is founded** by someone or by a group of people, they get it started, often by providing the necessary money. ○ *He founded the Missouri School of Journalism at University of Missouri.*

fragment /ˈfrægmənt/ **(fragments)**

NOUN A **fragment of** something is a small piece or part of it. ○ *There were fragments of metal in my shoulder.* ○ *She read everything, digesting every fragment of news.* ○ *glass fragments*

function /ˈfʌŋkʃ°n/ **(functions)**

NOUN The **function** of something or someone is the useful thing that they do or are intended to do. ○ *This enzyme serves various functions.* ○ *The main function of the merchant banks is to raise capital for industry.*

fund /ˈfʌnd/ **(funds, funding, funded)**

VERB When a person or organization **funds** something, they provide money for it. ○ *The Bush Foundation has funded a variety of faculty development programs.* ○ *The airport is being privately funded by a construction group.* ○ *a new, privately funded program*

grant /ˈgrænt/ **(grants, granting, granted)**

NOUN A **grant** is an amount of money that a government or other institution gives to an individual or to an organization for a particular purpose. ○ *They received a special grant to encourage research.* ○ *Unfortunately, my application for a grant was rejected.*

hereditary /hɪˈrɛdɪtɛri/

ADJECTIVE A **hereditary** characteristic or illness is passed on to a child from an earlier generation before it is born. ○ *Cystic fibrosis is most common fatal hereditary disease.* ○ *In men, hair loss is hereditary.*

home furnishing /hoʊm fɜrnɪʃɪn/ **(home furnishings)**
NOUN **Home furnishings** are the furniture, curtains, carpets, and decorations, such as pictures, in a room or house. ○ *To enable rental increases, you have to have luxurious home furnishings.*

hygiene /haɪdʒin/
NONCOUNT NOUN **Hygiene** is the practice of keeping yourself and your surroundings clean, especially in order to prevent illness or the spread of diseases. ○ *It was difficult to ensure hygiene when doctors were conducting numerous operations in quick succession.* ○ *a strict regime of cleanliness and personal hygiene*

hypothesis /haɪpɒθɪsɪs/ **(hypotheses)**
NOUN A **hypothesis** is an idea which is suggested as a possible explanation for a particular situation or condition, but which has not yet been proved to be correct. [FORMAL] ○ *Work will now begin to test the hypothesis in rats.* ○ *Different hypotheses have been put forward to explain why these foods are more likely to cause problems.*

implement /ɪmplɪmɛnt, -mənt/ **(implements, implementing, implemented)**
VERB If you **implement** something such as a plan, you ensure that what has been planned is done. ○ *The government promised to implement a new system to control financial loan institutions.* ○ *The report sets out strict inspection procedures to ensure that the recommendations are properly implemented.*

implication /ɪmplɪkeɪʃən/ **(implications)**
NOUN The **implications** of something are the things that are likely to happen as a result. ○ *the political implications of his decision* ○ *The low level of investment has serious implications for future economic growth.*

imply /ɪmplaɪ/ **(implies, implying, implied)**
VERB If you **imply that** something is the case, you say something that indicates that it is the case in an indirect way. ○ *"What exactly are you implying?" I demanded.* ○ *The government is implying the problem is not serious.*

indistinguishable /ɪndɪstɪŋgwɪʃəbəl/
ADJECTIVE If one thing is **indistinguishable from** another, the two things are so similar that it is difficult to know which is which. ○ *Replica weapons are indistinguishable from the real thing.*

industr ial /ɪndʌstriəl/
ADJECTIVE You use **industrial** to describe things which relate to or are used in industry. ○ *industrial machinery and equipment* ○ *a link between industrial chemicals and cancer*

inevitable /ɪnɛvɪtəbəl/
ADJECTIVE If something is **inevitable**, it is certain to happen and cannot be prevented or avoided. ○ *If the case succeeds, it is inevitable that other trials will follow.* ○ *The defeat had inevitable consequences for foreign policy.*

infancy /ɪnfənsi/
NONCOUNT NOUN **Infancy** is the period of your life when you are a very young child. ○ *the development of the mind from infancy onward* ○ *Only 50 percent of babies survive infancy in this region.*

infant /ɪnfənt/ **(infants)**
NOUN An **infant** is a baby or very young child. [FORMAL] ○ *vaccinations of newborn infants* ○ *the infant mortality rate*

inherit /ɪnhɛrɪt/ **(inherits, inheriting, inherited)**
VERB If you **inherit** a characteristic or quality, you are born with it, because your parents or ancestors also had it. ○ *We inherit many of our physical characteristics from our parents.* ○ *All sufferers from asthma have inherited a gene that makes them susceptible to the disease.* ○ *Stammering is probably an inherited defect.*

inspire /ɪnspaɪər/ **(inspires, inspiring, inspired)**
VERB If someone or something **inspires** you, they give you new ideas and a strong feeling of enthusiasm. ○ *In the 1960s, the electric guitar virtuosity of Jimi Hendrix inspired a generation.*

integrate /ɪntɪgreɪt/ **(integrates, integrating, integrated)**
VERB If you **integrate** one thing **with** another, or one thing **integrates with** another, the two things become closely linked or form part of a whole idea or system. You can also say that two things **integrate**. ○ *Integrating the British pound with other European currencies could cause difficulties.* ○ *Little attempt was made to integrate the parts into a coherent whole.*

interfere /ɪntərfɪər/ **(interferes, interfering, interfered)**
VERB Something that **interferes with** a situation, activity, or process has a damaging effect on it. ○ *Phytates interfere with your body's ability to absorb calcium.*

jack-of-all-trades /dʒæk əv ɔl treɪdz/ **(jacks-of-all-trades)**
NOUN If you refer to someone as a **jack-of-all-trades**, you mean that they are able to do a variety of different jobs. You are also often suggesting that they are not very good at any of these jobs. ○ *A celebrity jack-of-all-trades, he was an announcer, news broadcaster, weatherman, game-show host, talk-show personality, and an actor.*

key /ki/
ADJECTIVE The **key** person or thing in a group is the most important one. ○ *He is expected to be the key witness at the trial.*

lack /læk/
NONCOUNT NOUN If there is a **lack of** something, there is not enough of it or it does not exist at all. ○ *Despite his lack of experience, he got the job.* ○ *The charges were dropped for lack of evidence.*

layer /leɪər/ **(layers)**
NOUN A **layer** of a material or substance is a quantity or piece of it that covers a surface or that is between two other things. ○ *The eyelids are protective layers of skin.* ○ *holes appearing in the ozone layer over the polar regions*

legislate /lɛdʒɪsleɪt/ **(legislates, legislating, legislated)**
VERB When a government or state **legislates** something, it passes a new law to cause it to happen or exist. [FORMAL] ○ *attempts to legislate a national energy strategy*

legislation /lɛdʒɪsleɪʃᵊn/
NONCOUNT NOUN **Legislation** consists of a law or laws passed by a government. [FORMAL] ○ *The government has introduced draft legislation to increase the maximum penalty for car theft.* ○ *European legislation on copyright* ○ *changes to employment legislation* ○ *The government introduced legislation restricting trade union rights.* ○ *a highly complex piece of legislation*

legislative /lɛdʒɪsleɪtɪv/
ADJECTIVE **Legislative** means involving or relating to the process of making and passing laws. [FORMAL] ○ *Today's hearing was just the first step in the legislative process.* ○ *the country's highest legislative body*

liberal arts /lɪbərəl ɑrts/
NOUN At a university or college, **liberal arts** courses are on subjects such as history or literature rather than science, law, medicine, or business. ○ *The journalist says, "When you come out of a liberal arts background, you want to know why something is the way it is."* ○ *Firms now favor liberal arts degrees over the once-hot business degree.*

logo /loʊgoʊ/ **(logos)**
NOUN The **logo** of a company or organization is the special design or way of writing its name that it puts on all its products, notepaper, or advertisements. ○ *Staff should wear uniforms, and vehicles should bear company logos.* ○ *a red T-shirt with a logo on the front*

magnetic /mægnɛtɪk/
ADJECTIVE You use **magnetic** to describe something that is caused by or relates to the force of magnetism, the natural power of some objects and substances, especially iron, to attract other objects toward them. ○ *The moon exerts a magnetic pull on the Earth's water levels.* ○ *The electrically charged gas particles are affected by magnetic forces.*

mainstream /meɪnstrim/ **(mainstreams)**
NOUN People, activities, or ideas that are part of the **mainstream** are regarded as the most typical, normal, and conventional because they belong to the same group or system as most others of their kind. ○ *people outside the economic mainstream* ○ *This was the company's first step into the mainstream of scientific and commercial computing.* ○ *The show wanted to attract a mainstream audience.*

mandate /mændeɪt/ **(mandates)**
NOUN If someone is given a **mandate** to carry out a particular policy or task, they are given the official authority to do it. ○ *How much longer does the special prosecutor have a mandate to pursue this investigation?*

material /mətɪəriəl/ **(materials)**
NOUN A **material** is a solid substance. ○ *electrons in a conducting material such as a metal* ○ *the design of new absorbent materials* ○ *recycling of all materials*

motivate /moʊtɪveɪt/ **(motivates, motivating, motivated)**
VERB If you are **motivated** by something, it causes you to behave in a particular way. ○ *They are motivated by a need to achieve.* ○ *The crime was not politically motivated.*

no matter
PHRASE You use **no matter** in expressions such as "no matter how" and "no matter what" to say that something is true or happens in all circumstances. ○ *No matter what your age, you can lose weight by following this program.*

notable /noʊtəbᵊl/
ADJECTIVE Someone or something that is **notable** is important or interesting. ○ *The proposed new structure is notable not only for its height, but for its shape.* ○ *With a few notable exceptions, doctors are a pretty sensible bunch.*

novice /nɒvɪs/ **(novices)**
NOUN A **novice** is someone who has been doing a job or other activity for only a short time and so is not experienced at it. ○ *For expert and novice alike, it's a foolproof system.* ○ *Business novices learn the entrepreneurial ropes fast.*

objective /əbdʒɛktɪv/ **(objectives)**
NOUN Your **objective** is what you are trying to achieve. ○ *Our main objective was the recovery of the child safe and well.* ○ *Our objective is to become the number one digital corporation.*

obstruct /əbstrʌkt/ **(obstructs, obstructing, obstructed)**
VERB If something **obstructs** a road or passage, it blocks it, preventing anything from passing. ○ *Drivers who park their cars illegally, particularly obstructing traffic flow, deserve to be punished.*

obtain /əbteɪn/ **(obtains, obtaining, obtained)**
VERB To **obtain** something means to get it or achieve it. [FORMAL] ○ *Evans was trying to obtain a fake passport.* ○ *The perfect body has always been difficult to obtain.*

oppose /əpoʊz/ **(opposes, opposing, opposed)**
VERB If you **oppose** someone or **oppose** their plans or ideas, you disagree with what they want to do and try to prevent them from doing it. ○ *Mr. Taylor was not bitter towards those who had opposed him.* ○ *Many parents oppose bilingual education.*

option /ɒpʃᵊn/ **(options)**
NOUN An **option** is something that you can choose to do in preference to one or more alternatives. ○ *He argues that America and its allies are putting too much emphasis on the military option.* ○ *What other options do you have?*

organism /ˈɔrɡənɪzəm/ **(organisms)**

NOUN An **organism** is an animal or plant, especially one that is so small that you cannot see it without using a microscope. ○ *Not all chemicals normally present in living organisms are harmless.* ○ *insect-borne organisms that cause sleeping sickness*

partially /ˈpɑrʃəli/

ADVERB If something happens or exists **partially**, it happens or exists to some extent, but not completely. ○ *He was born with a rare genetic condition which has left him partially sighted.* ○ *partially hydrogenated oils*

perceive /pərˈsiv/ **(perceives, perceiving, perceived)**

VERB If you **perceive** someone or something **as** doing or being a particular thing, it is your opinion that they do this thing or that they are that thing. ○ *Stress is widely perceived as contributing to coronary heart disease.* ○ *Bioterrorism is perceived as a real threat in the United States.*

petition /pəˈtɪʃ°n/ **(petitions)**

NOUN A **petition** is a document signed by a lot of people that asks a government or other official group to do a particular thing. ○ *a petition signed by 4,500 people*

predatory /ˈprɛdətɔri/

ADJECTIVE **Predatory** animals live by killing other animals for food. ○ *predatory birds like the eagle*

prestigious /prɛˈstɪdʒəs, -ˈstidʒəs/

ADJECTIVE A **prestigious** institution, job, or activity is respected and admired by people. ○ *It's one of the best equipped and most prestigious schools in the country.*

prevail /prɪˈveɪl/ **(prevails, prevailing, prevailed)**

VERB If a situation, attitude, or custom **prevails** in a particular place at a particular time, it is normal or most common in that place at that time. ○ *A similar situation prevails in Canada.* ○ *Just how these ideas are expressed depends on the ideas prevailing in society at the time.*

prevalent /ˈprɛvələnt/

ADJECTIVE A condition, practice, or belief that is **prevalent** is common. ○ *This condition is more prevalent in women than in men.*

prevent /prɪˈvɛnt/ **(prevents, preventing, prevented)**

VERB To **prevent** something means to ensure that it does not happen. ○ *Further treatment will prevent cancer from developing.* ○ *We recognized the possibility and took steps to prevent it from happening.*

proliferation /prəˌlɪfəˈreɪʃ°n/

NONCOUNT NOUN The **proliferation** of something is a fast increase in its quantity. [FORMAL] ○ *the proliferation of nuclear weapons*

prolonged /prəˈlɔŋd/

ADJECTIVE A **prolonged** event or situation continues for a long time, or for longer than expected. ○ *a prolonged period of low interest rates*

prominent /ˈprɒmɪnənt/

ADJECTIVE Something that is **prominent** is very noticeable or is an important part of something else. ○ *Here the window plays a prominent part in the design.* ○ *Romania's most prominent independent newspaper*

pursuit /pərˈsut/

NONCOUNT NOUN The **pursuit of** something is the process of trying to understand and achieve it. ○ *a young man whose relentless pursuit of excellence is conducted with single-minded determination*

random /ˈrændəm/

ADJECTIVE A **random** sample or method is one in which all the people or things involved have an equal chance of being chosen. ○ *The survey used a random sample of two thousand people across the United States.* ○ *The competitors will be subject to random drug testing.*

range /ˈreɪndʒ/ **(ranges)**

NOUN A **range** is the complete group that is included between two points on a scale of measurement or quality. ○ *The average age range is between 35 and 55.* ○ *products available in this price range*

rational /ˈræʃən°l/

ADJECTIVE **Rational** decisions and thoughts are based on reason rather than on emotion. ○ *He's asking you to look at both sides of the case and come to a rational decision.* ○ *It was the most rational explanation at the time.*

reduce /rɪˈdus/ **(reduces, reducing, reduced)**

VERB If you **reduce** something, you make it smaller in size or amount, or less in degree. ○ *It reduces the risks of heart disease.* ○ *Consumption is being reduced by 25 percent.* ○ *The reduced consumer demand is also affecting company profits.*

reduction /rɪˈdʌkʃ°n/ **(reductions)**

NOUN When there is a **reduction in** something, it is made smaller. ○ *This morning's inflation figures show a reduction of 0.2 percent from 5.8 percent to 5.6.* ○ *Many companies have announced dramatic reductions in staff.* ○ *the reduction of inflation and interest rates*

refining /rɪˈfaɪnɪŋ/

NONCOUNT NOUN **Refining** is the process of making a substance pure by having all other substances removed from it. ○ *oil refining.*

reform /rɪfˈɔrm/ **(reforms, reforming, reformed)**
VERB If someone **reforms** something such as a law, social system, or institution, they change or improve it. ○ *his plans to reform the country's economy* ○ *A reformed party would have to win the approval of the people.* ○ *proposals to reform the tax system*

regard /rɪgˈɑrd/ **(regards, regarding, regarded)**
VERB If you **regard** someone or something **as** being a particular thing or as having a particular quality, you believe that they are that thing or have that quality. ○ *He was regarded as the most successful chancellor of modern times.* ○ *I regard creativity both as a gift and as a skill.* ○ *The vast majority of people would regard these proposals as unreasonable.*

regulate /rˈɛgyəleɪt/ **(regulates, regulating, regulated)**
VERB To **regulate** an activity or process means to control it, especially by means of rules. ○ *The powers of the Federal Trade Commission to regulate competition are increasing.* ○ *As we get older, the temperature-regulating mechanisms in the body tend to become a little less efficient.* ○ *regulating cholesterol levels*

relevance /rˈɛləvᵊns/
NONCOUNT NOUN Something's **relevance to** a situation or person is its importance or significance in that situation or to that person. ○ *Politicians' private lives have no relevance to their public roles.* ○ *There are additional publications of special relevance to new graduates.*

relevant /rˈɛləvᵊnt/
ADJECTIVE Something that is **relevant to** a situation or person is important or significant in that situation or to that person. ○ *Is socialism still relevant to people's lives?* ○ *We have passed all relevant information on to the police.*

renowned /rɪnˈaʊnd/
ADJECTIVE A person or place that is **renowned** is well known, usually because they do or have done something good. ○ *The university has a renowned toxicology center.*

restrict /rɪstrˈɪkt/ **(restricts, restricting, restricted)**
VERB If you **restrict** something, you put a limit on it in order to reduce it or prevent it from becoming too great. ○ *There is talk of raising the admission requirements to restrict the number of students on campus.* ○ *The French, I believe, restrict Japanese imports to a maximum of 3 percent of their market.*

restriction /rɪstrˈɪkʃn/ **(restrictions)**
NOUN A **restriction** is an official rule that limits what you can do or that limits the amount or size of something. ○ *Some restriction on funding was necessary.* ○ *the justification for this restriction of individual liberty* ○ *the lifting of restrictions on political parties*

retail apparel /rˈiteɪl əpˈærəl/
NONCOUNT NOUN **Retail apparel** is clothing that is made to be sold in stores. ○ *a chain of 104 fashion retail apparel stores*

reverse /rɪvˈɜrs/ **(reverses, reversing, reversed)**
VERB When someone or something **reverses** a decision, policy, or trend, they change it to the opposite decision, policy, or trend. ○ *They have made it clear they will not reverse the decision to increase prices.* ○ *The rise, the first in 10 months, reversed the downward trend in Belgium's jobless rate.*

sacrifice /sˈækrɪfaɪs/ **(sacrifices, sacrificing, sacrificed)**
VERB If you **sacrifice** something that is valuable or important, you give it up, usually to obtain something else for yourself or for other people. ○ *He is prepared to sacrifice ambition for other rewards.* ○ *She had sacrificed much to become a lawyer.*

sail through **(sails, sailing, sailed)**
PHRASAL VERB If someone or something **sails through** a difficult situation or experience, it is easy and successful for them. ○ *While she sailed through her exams, he struggled.*

scope /skˈoʊp/
NOUN The **scope of** an activity, topic, or piece of work is the whole area which it deals with or includes. ○ *Mr. Dobson promised to widen the organization's scope of activity.* ○ *the scope of a novel*

secondary /sˈɛkəndɛri/
ADJECTIVE If you describe something as **secondary**, you mean that it is less important than something else. ○ *The street erupted in a huge explosion, with secondary explosions in the adjoining buildings.* ○ *The actual damage to the brain cells is secondary to the damage caused to the blood supply.*

segment /sˈɛgmənt/ **(segments)**
NOUN A **segment of** something is one part of it, considered separately from the rest. ○ *the poorer segments of society* ○ *the third segment of his journey*

set forth **(sets forth, setting forth, set forth)**
PHRASAL VERB If you **set forth** a number of facts, beliefs, or arguments, you explain them in writing or speech in a clear, organized way. ○ *Dr. Mesibov set forth the basis of his approach to teaching students.*

site /sˈaɪt/ **(sites)**
NOUN A **site** is a piece of ground that is used for a particular purpose or where a particular thing happens. ○ *He worked on a building site.* ○ *a bat sanctuary with special nesting sites*

specimen /spˈɛsɪmɪn/ **(specimens)**
NOUN A **specimen of** something is an example of it which gives an idea of what the whole of it is like. ○ *Job applicants have to submit a specimen of handwriting.*

spectrum /spˈɛktrəm/ **(spectra, spectrums)**
NOUN A **spectrum** is a range of a particular type of thing. ○ *She'd seen his moods range across the emotional spectrum.* ○ *Politicians across the political spectrum have denounced the act.* ○ *The term "special needs" covers a wide spectrum of problems.*

speed reading /spid ridɪŋ/
NOUN **Speed reading** is reading something very fast. ○ *JFK, one of the first politicians to understand the benefits of speed reading, managed 1,000 words a minute.*

spur of the moment
PHRASE If you do something **on the spur of the moment**, you do it suddenly, without planning it beforehand. ○ *They admitted they had taken a vehicle on the spur of the moment.*

steep /stip/ **(steeper, steepest)**
ADJECTIVE A **steep** increase or decrease in something is a very big increase or decrease. ○ *Consumers are rebelling at steep price increases.* ○ *Many smaller emerging Asian economies are suffering their steepest economic declines for half a century.*

strain /streɪn/ **(strains)**
NOUN A **strain of** a germ, plant, or other organism is a particular type of it. ○ *Every year new strains of influenza develop.*

strategy /strætədʒi/ **(strategies)**
NOUN A **strategy** is a general plan or set of plans intended to achieve something, especially over a long period. ○ *Next week, health officials gather in Amsterdam to agree on a strategy for controlling malaria.* ○ *a customer-led marketing strategy.*

strike /straɪk/ **(strikes, striking, struck)**
VERB If something that is falling or moving **strikes** something, it hits it. ○ *the fire that began when the roof was struck by lightning*

subsequently /sʌbsɪkwəntli/
ADVERB You use **subsequently** to introduce something that happened or existed after the time or event that has just been referred to. [FORMAL] ○ *He subsequently worked on Boeing's 747, 767, and 737 jetliner programs.*

suitable /sutəbəl/
ADJECTIVE Someone or something that is **suitable for** a particular purpose or occasion is right or acceptable for it. ○ *Employers usually decide within five minutes whether someone is suitable for the job.* ○ *The organization must provide suitable accommodation for the family.*

survey /sɜrveɪ/ **(surveys)**
NOUN If you carry out a **survey**, you try to find out detailed information about a lot of different people or things, usually by asking people a series of questions. ○ *The council conducted a survey of the uses to which farm buildings are put.* ○ *According to the survey, overall world trade has also slackened.*

sustainable /səsteɪnəbəl/
ADJECTIVE You use **sustainable** to describe the use of natural resources when this use is kept at a steady level that is not likely to damage the environment. ○ *the management, conservation, and sustainable development of forests* ○ *Try to buy wood that you know has come from a sustainable source.*

switch /swɪtʃ/ **(switches, switching, switched)**
VERB If you **switch to** something different, for example to a different system, task, or subject of conversation, you change to it from what you were doing or saying before. ○ *Estonia is switching to a market economy.* ○ *The law would encourage companies to switch from coal to cleaner fuels.*

symbol /sɪmbəl/ **(symbols)**
NOUN A **symbol of** something such as a number or a sound is a shape or design that is used to represent it. ○ *One wall was covered in pencil scribblings, all kinds of symbols and numbers which to me were unintelligible.* ○ *mathematical symbols and operations*

take for granted
PHRASE If you **take something for granted**, you believe that it is true or accept it as normal without thinking about it. ○ *Respiration controls our life and yet it is something we take for granted.*

technique /tɛknik/ **(techniques)**
NOUN A **technique** is a particular method of doing an activity, usually a method that involves practical skills. ○ *tests performed using a new technique* ○ *developments in the surgical techniques employed* ○ *traditional bread making techniques*

term /tɜrm/ **(terms)**
NOUN A **term** is a word or expression with a specific meaning, especially one which is used in relation to a particular subject. ○ *Myocardial infarction is the medical term for a heart attack.*

territory /tɛrətɔri/ **(territories)**
NOUN **Territory** is land that is controlled by a particular country or ruler. ○ *None of the former Spanish territories enjoyed long periods of independence.*

testify /tɛstɪfaɪ/ **(testifies, testifying, testified)**
VERB When someone **testifies** in a court of law, they give a statement of what they saw someone do or what they know of a situation, after having promised to tell the truth. ○ *Several eyewitnesses testified that they saw the officers hit Miller in the face.* ○ *Eva testified to having seen Herndon with his gun on the stairs.* ○ *He hopes to have his 12-year prison term reduced by testifying against his former coworkers.*

theory /θɪəri/ **(theories)**
NOUN A **theory** is a formal idea or set of ideas that is intended to explain something. ○ *Einstein formulated the Theory of Relativity in 1905.*

therefore /ðɛərfɔr/
ADVERB You use **therefore** to introduce a logical result or conclusion. ○ *Muscle cells need lots of fuel and therefore burn lots of calories.* ○ *We expect to continue to gain new customers and therefore also market shares.*

thesis /θiːsɪs/ (theses)

NOUN A **thesis** is an idea or theory that is expressed as a statement and is discussed in a logical way. ○ *This thesis does not stand up to close inspection.*

trait /treɪt/ (traits)

NOUN A **trait** is a particular characteristic, quality, or tendency that someone or something has. ○ *The study found that some alcoholics had clear personality traits showing up early in childhood.* ○ *Do we inherit traits such as agility and sporting excellence, and musical or artistic ability?*

transformation /trænsfərmeɪʃⁿn/ (transformations)

NOUN A **transformation** is the complete change of something into something else. ○ *one of the most astonishing economic transformations seen since the Second World War* ○ *After 1959, the Spanish economy underwent a profound transformation.*

trigger /trɪgər/ (triggers, triggering, triggered)

VERB If something **triggers** an event or situation, it causes it to begin to happen or exist. ○ *the incident that triggered the outbreak of the First World War* ○ *The current recession was triggered by a slump in consumer spending.*

tuition /tuɪʃⁿn/

NONCOUNT NOUN **Tuition** is the money paid by students to the school or college that they attend. ○ *You need to pay your tuition and to support yourself financially.*

undergo /ʌndərgoʊ/ (undergoes, undergoing, underwent, undergone)

VERB If a person or thing **undergoes** something necessary or unpleasant, it happens to them. ○ *New recruits have been undergoing training in recent weeks.* ○ *When cement powder is mixed with water, it undergoes a chemical change and hardens.*

undertaking /ʌndərteɪkɪŋ/ (undertakings)

NOUN An **undertaking** is a task or job, especially a large or difficult one. ○ *Organizing the show has been a massive undertaking.*

unorthodox /ʌnɔrθədɒks/

ADJECTIVE If you describe someone's behavior, beliefs, or customs as **unorthodox**, you mean that they are different from what is generally accepted. ○ *The reality-based show followed the unorthodox lives of Ozzy, his wife, daughter, and son.*

utilize /yutɪlaɪz/ (utilizes, utilizing, utilized)

VERB If you **utilize** something, you use it. [FORMAL] ○ *Sound engineers utilize a range of techniques to enhance the quality of the recordings.* ○ *Minerals can be absorbed and utilized by the body in a variety of different forms.*

vary /vɛəri/ (varies, varying, varied)

VERB If things **vary**, they are different from each other in size, amount, or degree. ○ *Assessment practices vary in different schools or colleges.* ○ *The text varies from the earlier versions.* ○ *Different writers will prepare to varying degrees.*

venture /vɛntʃər/ (ventures)

NOUN A **venture** is a project or activity that is new. ○ *a Russian-American joint venture*

verify /vɛrɪfaɪ/ (verifies, verifying, verified)

VERB If you **verify** something, you check that it is true by careful examination or investigation. ○ *continued testing to verify the accuracy of the method* ○ *A clerk simply verifies that the payment and invoice amount match.*

vertical /vɜrtɪkⁿl/

ADJECTIVE Something that is **vertical** stands or points straight up. ○ *The price variable is shown on the vertical axis, with quantity demanded on the horizontal axis.* ○ *The gadget can be attached to any vertical or near vertical surface.*

via /vaɪə, viə/

PREPOSITION If you do something **via** a particular means or person, you do it by making use of that means or person. ○ *The technology to allow relief workers to contact the outside world via satellite already exists.* ○ *Translators can now work from home, via electronic mail systems.*

volume /vɒlyum/ (volumes)

NOUN A **volume** is one book or journal in a series of books or journals. The abbreviation vol. is used in written notes and bibliographies. ○ *the first volume of his autobiography* ○ *The article appeared in volume 41 of the journal Communication Education.*

vulnerable /vʌlnərəbⁿl/

ADJECTIVE If someone or something is **vulnerable to** something, they have some weakness or disadvantage which makes them more likely to be harmed or affected by that thing. ○ *People with high blood pressure are especially vulnerable to diabetes.*

wane /weɪn/ (wanes, waning, waned)

VERB If something **wanes**, it becomes gradually weaker or less, often so that it eventually disappears. ○ *While his interest in these sports began to wane, a passion for lacrosse developed.*

whereas /wɛəræz/

CONJUCTION You use **whereas** to introduce a comment which contrasts with what is said in the main clause. ○ *Pensions are linked to inflation, whereas they should be linked to the cost of living.* ○ *Whereas the population of working age increased by 1 million between 1981 and 1986, today it is barely growing.*

AUDIO SCRIPT

Listening, Part 1

Questions 1–5

Track 1 [page 20]

Listen as a student consults with a university employee.

Student: Is this the bursar's office?

Employee: Yes, it is. Can I help you?

Student: I need to register for next semester's classes, but my advisor told me I have a hold on my account and can't register.

Employee: Well, then it must be a financial hold if your advisor told you to come to the bursar's office. If it had been an academic hold, you would have to go to the dean's office. Let me check. Can you spell your last name for me, or do you know your ID number?

Student: It's probably easier if I give you my ID number. It's 66011406.

Employee: Ah, here you are. That's right. You owe $32.00 for parking tickets. Your license number is 76841, correct?

Student: Oh no! I paid that last week. I have the receipt somewhere in my backpack. Here it is.

Employee: Let me see the receipt. You're right. My apologies. Sometimes the interoffice emails take a few days to get updated into our system. While you're here, Mr. Hatayadom, did I pronounce your name correctly?

Student: Close enough. I'm used to it by now. The stress is on the *DOM*, HatayaDOM. It's equally hard to spell and pronounce!

Employee: I see you're not on the monthly tuition payment plan. Many students pay this way, so they don't have to come up with so much money all at once.

Student: Can international students pay this way?

Employee: Of course. There's a ninety dollar annual service fee to the company—we use College Payment Services, a local company—and then you pay them monthly. You then won't be billed from us any longer. They pay us, and you work out a monthly payment plan with them. But, it's totally up to you. I have their brochure if you want to take it with you. It explains how it works and how to contact the company.

Student: Sure. I'll read it over and discuss it with my parents. Umm, are you sure the hold has been removed from my account?

Employee: Take a look. If you had a hold, there would be an X in the hold column. It's empty.

Student: OK. Thanks. Now I have to hope my advisor is still in her office to approve my course choices.

Employee: Good luck Mr. Hatayadom, and feel free to stop by any time.

Student: Thanks, but let's hope I won't have to.

Track 2 [page 21]

Listen again to part of the passage. Then answer the question.

Employee: Can you spell your last name for me, or do you know your ID number?

Student: It's probably easier if I give you my ID number.

Why does the student say this?

Student: It's probably easier if I give you my ID number.

Questions 6 through 11

Track 3 [page 22]

Listen to a lecture in a genetics class.

Professor: Welcome to Genetics 101. I'm sure most of you have had some class work in your high school biology class with genetics: why some people have blue eyes, why some have curly hair, and so on. This course will examine the relationship between genetics and biochemistry and the impact on medicine, disease, and agriculture today. I know that some of you are taking this course to fulfill your science elective and have no intention of majoring in one of the natural sciences, whereas this course is required for biology majors. I hope to make this course interesting to all of you nevertheless. I predict that you will find many of the lectures and case studies extremely interesting and relevant to your lives.

I hope you've all read chapter one in our textbook. We begin, of course, with the father of genetics, Gregor Johann Mendel, the Austrian botanist and monk. I'm sure you recall his experiments with the breeding of garden peas led to the development of this field of study. In case you're a little rusty, let me remind you of his experiments. He studied the inheritance of seven distinct traits in garden pea plants. These traits included seed shape, were they smooth or wrinkled, and plant height, were they tall or short plants?

He then—remember he was a monk, so he was a very patient man—bred and crossbred hundreds of plants and observed the characteristics of each successive generation. Like all organisms that reproduce, pea plants produce their offspring through the union of special cells called gametes. In pea plants, a male gamete, or pollen grain, combines with a female gamete, or egg cell, to form a seed.

Mendel concluded that plant traits are handed down through hereditary elements in the gametes. These elements we now call genes. Each gene can have slightly different information related to one trait. We call these variants alleles. He reasoned that each plant receives a pair of alleles for each trait, one allele from each of its parents. Based on his experiments, he concluded that if a plant inherits two different alleles for one trait, one allele will be dominant and the other will be recessive. The trait of the dominant allele will be visible in the plant. For example, the allele for smooth seeds is dominant, and the allele for wrinkled seeds is recessive. A plant that inherits a different copy of each allele will have round seeds.

Now, most of Mendel's theories have been proved although some exceptions have been found. I'm going to get off track for a couple of minutes to discuss the difficulties of predicting red hair. Since I'm a carrot-top myself, I find the issue near and dear to my heart. The myth that redheads might die off in the near future has drawn considerable attention. Due to the recessive and not dominant nature of red hair, it takes two carriers to have a red-headed child. You can have brown hair but still be carrying the recessive allele for red hair. Let's look at some charts. If both parents are carriers but not redheads, there is a 25% chance of producing redheads. If one parent had red hair and the other is a carrier, there's a 50-50 chance. If both parents have red hair, then all offspring will be red headed. I'll share with you that I have two children, and one has brown hair. Can you tell me what color hair my wife has? It's actually a tricky question, and I'll explain why in Wednesday's class.

Track 4 [page 23]

Listen again to part of the passage. Then answer the question.

Professor: I'm sure you recall his experiments with the breeding of garden peas led to the development of this field of study. In case you're a little rusty, let me remind you of his experiments. He studied the inheritance of seven distinct traits in garden pea plants. These traits included seed shape, were they smooth or wrinkled and plant height, were they tall or short plants?

What does the professor mean when he says this?

Professor: In case you're a little rusty…

Questions 12-17

Track 5 [page 24]

Listen to a discussion from a philosophy class.

Professor: Remember we're leaving for Brook Farm this Saturday at 8:30 A.M. It should take us about four hours to get there.

Student 1: But professor? I know I read it burned down.

Professor: Yes, that's partially correct. The central building burned down in 1846, and all that remains of the community who lived there from 1841 to 1846 are cellar holes.

Student 2: So if that's all that's left, why are we going?

Professor: Good question. Today there is a new push to sow the seeds for a New Brook Farm, one that will support sustainable farming and community education. I've been asked, since I'm a Transcendentalist scholar, if my students and I would be interested in taking the lead on this new venture.

Student 3: With everything we've been studying about Transcendentalists, I think the founding fathers would delight in this rebirth.

Professor: Agreed. And there will be a connection with children from area schools as well. So those of you who are getting a teaching certificate can perhaps help us out here.

Student 4: Didn't I read that the land though wasn't suitable for farming, and since they embraced physical labor, the lack of farming led to the downfall of Brook Farm?

Professor: That's partially correct. One of the biggest issues back in the 1840s for them was a lack of water power. Today that won't be an issue. The site is on the city water line, and there will be plenty of water for limited farming. Remember it will be farming with an emphasis on school-aged children, so no large machinery.

Student 2: Will it be organic?

Professor: I'm afraid that would be too expensive. It will be crops that you would find at a local farmer's market such as herbs and whatever the public seems to want.

Student 1: How many people actually lived at Brook Farm?

Professor: They began with 15. Each member worked several hours a day on the farm so they could be close to nature. They believed that the physical world is secondary to the spiritual world, but they wanted to be financially self-sufficient. Some wealthy authors of the day, including Nathaniel Hawthorne, lived there briefly, but the idea was that that the community would live off what it produced. It lasted only six years and never had more than 120 members at one time.

Student 2: Were they all philosophers?

Professor: Yes, in the sense that they all believed in Transcendentalism as a philosophy for life, encompassing literature, religion, and social issues. Don't forget, it wasn't all work. After work and dinner, they had plenty of time for music, dancing, card playing, dramatic readings, costume parties, sledding, and skating.

Student 3: I think the young students would enjoy seeing us dressed in costumes, such as typical clothing of the 1840s.

Student 4: And we should probably come up with a list of herbs or other small plants and vegetables that wouldn't be hard to grow quickly.

Professor: I'm glad to see you're getting excited about the project. Remember to read chapter 3 before Saturday, and bring with you a notebook or portable computer and wear comfortable clothing.

Track 6 [page 25]

Listen again to part of the passage. Then answer the question.

Professor: And there will be a connection with children from area schools as well. So those of you who are getting a teaching certificate can perhaps help us out here.

Why does the professor say this?

Professor: Those of you who are getting a teaching certificate can perhaps help us out here.

Questions 18 through 22

Track 7 [page 26]

Listen to a conversation between a student and a professor.

Student: I was wondering if you had the time to go over some ideas I have for my persuasive speech. My presentation is a week from Thursday.

Professor: Sure. This is a good time. It's my office hour. Come in and have a seat. What ideas have you come up with?

Student: I know you told us to stay away from the usual topics, like why everyone should vote, but I'm afraid the two ideas I have aren't so original.

Professor: Perhaps you misunderstood me. I didn't say the idea has to be original. What I did say is if you choose a topic that most students already have an opinion about, it's hard to get them to be open-minded to your speech. Do you remember I suggested you can do a quick paper survey to see where the class stands? If you were doing why everyone should vote, for example, you could just hand out a piece of paper to everyone and ask "Are you planning to vote in the next election?" If you find that most of the class is planning NOT to vote, it will affect what you present. So what have you come up with?

Student: One is that we should stop drinking bottled water and the second is that the shuttle bus from the subway to campus should run later on the weekends.

Professor: Two good topics. Let me hear your research on both.

Student: With bottled water, I thought I'd begin with a rhetorical question—like you suggest. How many of you have bought a bottle of water in the past month? I'm sure many hands will go up. I then will discuss the research about the amount of plastic from water bottles in landfills and in the ocean and how that plastic will remain for the next couple of hundred years.

Professor: Remember those facts and statistics need to be recent and reliable and tell us where you got the information from. What will you discuss after you give the facts and statistics? You'll need to have expert testimony. Since it's a persuasive speech, you'll need to be clear on what is it you want the students to do. How can they change their lives without making the expectation too difficult to enact?

Student: I'm good with the research part. I'm still grappling with the enactment part. I know it's easy to carry around a bottle of water. I don't want to ask them to do something they're not going to do. I think I might have a good idea. I've been talking with the bookstore about ordering new water bottles made from special new material that keep drinks cold or warm and have our school's logo imprinted on them. I might be able to get some at a steep discount since it was my idea, and then I could hand them out. I'm hoping the student government activities fund will give me the money to buy them.

Professor: Freebies are always good. That topic is sounding better and better. Tell me about the second one.

Student: I don't know if you know that the shuttle bus stops running at 11 p.m. on weekends. That means we have to leave downtown no later than 10:30 to make sure we're at the shuttle stop by 11. That's ridiculously early.

Professor: Do you have any idea approximately how many students would like to take a later shuttle? This topic is less academic, but it certainly is relevant to our class. You could find out what time other colleges and universities in our area stop running their shuttles, and you could have the class sign a petition. That's an easy expectation.

Student: Now I'm even more confused because I feel I have two good topics! Thanks for your advice and for listening.

Professor: My pleasure.

Track 8 [page 27]

Listen again to part of the passage. Then answer the question.

Professor: Tell me about the second one.

Student: I don't know if you know that the shuttle bus stops running at 11 p.m. on weekends. That means we have to leave downtown no later than 10:30 to make sure we're at the shuttle stop by 11.

Why does the student say this?

Questions 23 through 28

Track 9 [page 28]

Listen to a lecture in an American history class.

Professor: Using ice to preserve food led to the nineteenth-century development of the ice box. I recall my grandparents would say "icebox" instead of refrigerator. OK, but I'm sure none of you know who first came up with the idea of a refrigerator. Anyone know? Well, the entrepreneur was a Boston businessman named Frederic Tudor, who became known as the "Ice King." A passing remark at a party in 1805 gave him the idea of exploiting one of New England's few natural resources—the ice on its ponds.

By 1825 Tudor and his partner Nathaniel Wyeth had perfected an ice-cutting machine that mechanized the process of cutting slabs of ice. Through trial and error they worked out the best methods for building and insulating ships to transport the ice as well as icehouses to store it. The earlier underground icehouses suffered a minimum 60 percent seasonal loss due to melting. Inside Tudor's heavy, double wood walls with sawdust insulation, loss from melting was only eight percent.

In 1833, Tudor sent one of his ships with 180 tons of ice from Boston to Calcutta, crossing the equator twice in a voyage of four months and arriving with the ice still frozen. Although the main export markets were the American South and Caribbean islands, Tudor shipped his product all over the world and found plenty of customers locally in Boston as well. In the 1850s, Tudor's company exported up to 150,000 tons of ice a year while at the same time developing an American market.

Tudor's accomplishments helped make possible the icebox—an American word—which by 1860 had become a domestic must-have in American homes all across the country. These large wooden boxes on legs were lined with tin and zinc and interlined with charcoal, cork, sawdust, or straw. Many were handsome pieces of furniture. A large block of ice was held in a tray or compartment near the top of the box. Cold air circulated down and around storage compartments in the lower section. More expensive models had spigots for draining ice water from a catch pan or holding tank. Cheaper models used a drip pan that was placed under the box and had to be emptied at least daily. The users had to replace the melted ice, normally by obtaining new ice from an iceman.

Back to my grandparents. They regaled me with stories of their iceman who delivered blocks of ice to their home by horse and buggy. We're talking about the early 1900s until refrigeration became prevalent in the 1930s when refrigerators began using electricity instead of ice to keep their contents cold.

Ice boxes helped to improve the American diet and lengthened the season for fruits and vegetables. Meat could be preserved longer without salting, pickling, spicing, sun drying, or smoking. Ice cream became a popular at home treat rather than a rare luxury. Americans began putting ice in their drinks even though European visitors were appalled. Even iced tea, to the dismay of the hot tea-loving British, appeared before the Civil War.

Track 10 [page 29]

Listen again to part of the passage. Then answer the question.

Professor: The users had to replace the melted ice, normally by obtaining new ice from an iceman. Back to my grandparents. They regaled me with stories of their iceman who delivered blocks of ice to their home by horse and buggy.

How does the professor feel about the stories?

Questions 29 through 34

Track 11 [page 30]

Listen to a lecture in an economics class.

Professor: Today we're going to begin our study of game theory. It's probably one of the most seemingly simple but yet complex economic theories. This so-called branch of economics uses math to study strategy. In game theory, any situation, such as a board game, sports, a game of luck, or military decisions, are called games. What I'm saying is that game theory is used to study any situation in which more than one person makes choices.

The players are not always even people. Players can be people, companies, or even armies. Each player wants something. For example, a company wants to make as much money as it can or a country wants to win a war. Sometimes the players work cooperatively, but oftentimes they compete against one another.

One well-known game is called the prisoner's dilemma. It's an imaginary situation that explains why people do not cooperate in real life. Here's how the dilemma works. Imagine this situation. The police catch two criminals after they have committed a crime. The police do not know which person committed the crime and which one just helped. They question the two in separate cells. Each prisoner can either stay silent or blame the crime on the other person. If both stay silent, they go to jail for only six months. If one betrays, and the other stays silent, the one that stays silent goes to jail for 10 years, and the other one does not go to jail at all. If they both betray each other, they each go jail for 2 years. No matter what happens, the prisoners will never see each other again.

If you're a prisoner in this situation, and you care only about yourself, the way to get the smallest sentence is to betray the other prisoner. No matter what, you get a shorter sentence when you betray than when you don't. If the other prisoner stays silent and doesn't betray, then betraying means you do not go to jail at all instead of going for 6 months. If the other prisoner betrays, then betraying lets you go to jail for 2 years instead of 10 years. In other words, it's always best for you to betray even though the two of you would be better off if you both remained silent. But can you take a chance that the other prisoner will stay silent? We use the term "dominant strategy" to mean that strategy that is always the best thing for you to

do. In this case, it's betraying the other prisoner no matter what the other prisoner does.

This situation is like many other situations in the real world. For example, if two countries are trying to decide whether to make new weapons, they are better off if neither country does. But sometimes the countries are in the same situation as the prisoners; each country cares only about itself, and it's better off if it "betrays" the other country by making weapons.

The prisoner's dilemma does not have the same result if some of the details are different. If the prisoners—or countries can talk with each other and plan for the future, they might both decide to cooperate and not betray each other because they hope that decision will make the other country help them in the future. In game theory, this is called a "repeated game." If the players are altruistic, that is they care about each other, they might be OK with going to jail, so they can help the other person. We will continue this topic next class with some other dilemmas and some other mathematical models. Answer the problem set that's assigned on the syllabus.

Track 12 [page 32]

Listen again to part of the passage. Then answer the question.

Professor: But sometimes the countries are in the same situation as the prisoners; each country cares only about itself, and it's better off if it "betrays" the other country by making weapons.

What does the professor mean when she says this?

Professor: … and it's better off if it betrays the other country …

Speaking

Track 13 [page 34]

1. You will hear a question about a familiar topic. Listen to the question, and then prepare a response. You will have 15 seconds to prepare a response and 45 seconds to speak. You can take notes on the main points of a response.

   What is your most treasured possession? Use reasons and details to support your response.

Track 14 [page 35]

2. You will be asked your opinion about a familiar topic. Listen to the question, and then prepare your response. You will have 15 seconds to prepare a response and 45 seconds to speak. You can take notes on the main points of a response.

Some students choose to attend a large university with thousands of students. Others choose to attend a small one. Would you prefer to attend a large university or a small one? Use reasons and details to support your response.

Track 15 [page 36]

3. You will read a short passage and then listen to a conversation about the same topic. You will then answer a question about about them. You will have 45 seconds to read the passage. You can take notes on the main points of the reading passage.

Listen to two students discuss the announcement.

Man: Did you get the announcement? It went out via email a few minutes ago.

Woman: Yeah. I got a text also. How long do you think we're going to be stuck at the hotel?

Man: I wouldn't say "stuck." It's air conditioned, there is cable TV, and there's an indoor pool. Housekeeping even cleans the rooms every day!

Woman: I know it's much nicer in the hotel than in Shaw, but I'd still rather be in the dorm. It's way too inconvenient to go back to the hotel between classes, and we had to leave so quickly I don't have most of my clothes or books. I've worn the same sweater for three days in a row, and I'm afraid my grades will slip this semester. The worst part is I don't have my notes to study for this week's chemistry test.

Man: All of my teachers have been so nice about it. One put books on reserve in the library, another handed out notes from all earlier lectures, and my economics professor has invited those of us in the hotel to his house for dinner.

Woman: Aren't you the lucky one. No wonder you're not complaining! I'm hoping that we can back in the dorm today or tomorrow to get some stuff out.

Now answer the following question:

How do these students feel about staying in the hotel? Explain the reasons they give.

Track 16 [page 38]

4. You will read a short passage and then listen to a conversation about the same topic. You will then answer a question about about them. You will have 45 seconds to read the passage. You can take notes on the main points of the reading passage.

Listen to the passage.

Professor: So we've been discussing whether or not parents should sleep with their children in the same bed. Those of you from cultures where this practice is common may find the American obsession with this question—should parents sleep with their children or shouldn't they—somewhat amusing.

Pressure on parents not to sleep with babies in the United States comes from many sources, such as relatives and other parents. Even some pediatricians discourage the practice, for they fear the parents will roll over and suffocate the child. A commonly held American belief has been that children, beginning in infancy, need to learn to take care of their own needs; therefore, sleeping with a parent interferes with this ability.

However, there is a small but growing movement in the U.S. that encourages co-sleeping arrangements. These parents turn to Japan as an example of successful co-sleeping for hundreds of years. Dr. Harkness of the University of Connecticut conducted cross-cultural studies and found no correlation between having babies sleep alone and developing a sense of autonomy.

Now answer the following question:

How does the information in the listening passage add to what is explained in the reading passage?

Track 17 [page 40]

5. You will listen to part of a lecture. You can take notes on the main points of the listening passage.

Professor: And now we move onto the next machine. Today we're all familiar with this relatively new one in front of us. This CAT Scan, or CT Scan, stands for Computed Tomography scan. It is a medical imaging method that employs tomography. Tomography is the process of generating a two-dimensional image of a slice or section through a three-dimensional object, a tomogram. Undergoing a CAT scan is a painless procedure. The CAT scan uses digital geometry processing to generate a three-dimensional image of the inside of an object. Many pictures of the same area are taken from many angles and then placed together to produce a 3-D image. The Greek word *tomos* means to slice and the Greek word *graphein* means to write. Inside a CAT scan there is an X-ray detector that can see hundreds of levels of density. It can see tissues inside a solid organ. The data are transmitted to a computer, which builds up a 3-D cross-sectional picture of the part of the body and displays it on the screen. CAT scans are very useful in getting a very detailed 3-D image of certain parts of the body, such as soft tissues, the pelvis, blood vessels, the lungs, the brain, the abdomen, and bones.

The first patient brain scan using X-ray computed tomography—the CAT scan—was done on October 1, 1971 in England. Since its introduction in the 1970s, the CAT scan has become an important tool in place of traditional X-rays due to its production of superior images that often detect disease at an earlier stage than the traditional X-ray can. The usage of these scans has increased dramatically over the last two decades. An estimated 72 million scans were performed last year in the U.S., an increase of 2,600 percent from 1980, due to improved technology, speed, and a greater number of machines, thereby lowering the cost.

What is not commonly known is that the Beatles, perhaps the most famous musical band in history, funded the research to build the CAT scan prototype. The CAT scan invention earned the 1979 Nobel Prize in Medicine.

Now answer the following question:

How does the professor explain what a CAT scan does and how it was funded?

Track 18 [page 41]

6. You will hear a conversation.

Woman: Hey, Scott, are you going to take the pre-externship course next semester?

Man: I thought we had to. Didn't Professor Chang say all Human Service majors have to take it the semester before we do the senior externship?

Woman: That's my problem. It's a one-credit course, and I was going to take 18 credits next semester. If I take it, I'll have 19. Then I'll have to pay for the extra credit.

Man: Right, 15 is a full load, but we can take 18 without an extra charge. Why were you planning to take 18?

Woman: Oh…My first semester I had to take developmental math for no credit, so I'm three credits behind. I know I could take a course in summer school, but I'd have to pay for that also.

Man: I heard Professor Chang say the course helps you in getting the externship, doing a résumé, researching sites, applying, and interviewing. If you go see her, maybe she'll let you sit in on the course without paying for it since you don't need the credit to graduate. It would be like auditing it. Ask her. She seems really nice.

Woman: I could do that or I could take the 18 credits in the semester when we're doing the externship, but I'm afraid we'll be too busy with doing the

externship off campus. I have to factor in travel time plus the 100 hours of the externship itself.

Now answer the following question:

The speakers discuss two possible solutions to the woman's problem. Describe the problem and the two solutions. Then explain what you think the woman should do and why.

Writing 1
Track 19 [page 45]

Listen to the passage.

Professor: Although kids everywhere may delight in the fact that bees are no longer stinging them on playgrounds and in their backyards as frequently as they used to, the decline in the honeybee populations in the U.S. and around the globe signals a major environmental imbalance that can have far-reaching implications for our agricultural food supply.

The world first took notice in 2006 as beekeepers and scientists began reporting an alarming decline in the bee populations on a number of continents. You might ask why were so many of us caught off guard? Was it a sudden disappearance, or had bee populations been slowly decreasing? Actually the answer is that the numbers dramatically fell suddenly in the middle of the decade. At that time some rather weird and peculiar explanations began circulating. What was causing the bee deaths?

A recent gathering of leading bee biologists yielded no agreement as to the single cause, but most agree that a combination of factors, with one major culprit, is causing the decline. The effects of global warming causing more viruses, as well as radiation from the rapid growth of cell phones, contribute to the bee demise. Most scientists place most of the blame squarely on pesticides that affect the central nervous system of the insect, causing death. Although there are laws in place that restrict the dose of these pesticides, evidence suggests that even low doses can produce severe problems, impacting bees' memory and ability to return home to the hive.

Now answer the following question:

How does the information in the listening passage cast doubt on the information presented in the reading passage?

Listening 2

Questions 1-5

Track 20 [page 76]

Listen as a student consults with a professor.

Student: Hi, Professor Brown. I'm Lauren Klee. You've been assigned to me as an advisor since Professor Jenkinson left. Do you have a few minutes to discuss some questions I have about my major?

Professor: Hello Lauren. Come in and have a seat. Please tell me more about your situation, and we'll try to sort it out. What is your major right now?

Student: Well, currently I'm a first semester junior majoring in biology. I do want to apply to medical school, but I've been finding some of the advanced science courses a grind. I thought maybe I should switch to history or business, since those majors might be easier for me.

Professor: If you switched now, when would you take all the science prerequisites for med school?

Student: I've already taken a lot of them. I thought if I switched, I could bring up my GPA and have a better shot at med school.

Professor: Oh, you believe the nonscience courses are easier. Perhaps you're right. What is your GPA?

Student: A 3.0.

Professor: Hmm. I'm sure you know it's very competitive to get into med school. Since you've already taken a lot of the prereqs, why not remain a biology major? If you switched now, would you be able to graduate in four years? Don't medical schools prefer their applicants to be science majors?

Student: Not necessarily. What they look at is one, your GPA, two, how you do on the entrance exams and three, that you've taken all the prereqs. Some students do that after they graduate. And I did check out exactly how many courses I'd need if I switched majors. You know since the college started using its new advising program, I can use the "What If" link on the college website and see exactly how many and which courses I would need if I switched my major, to say history or business.

Professor: And how many required courses would you have left for each of those?

Student: Seven for history and eight for business.

Professor: Then it shouldn't be a problem since you have a year and a half left. I do suggest you make sure to take all the required premed courses however. Some of them are not offered every semester.

Student: For sure. Thanks so much.

Questions 6 through 11

Track 21 [page 78]

Listen to a discussion in a fashion design class.

Professor: As I look around today, I see many of you are wearing flip flops even though you're not going to the beach or a swimming pool. I'm sure most of you have no idea about their evolution, and you think they were invented as pool shoes. Throughout the world they have a variety of other names, such as zori, thongs, and jandals. These open-toed sandals consist of a flat sole held loosely on the foot by a Y-shaped strap that passes between the first and second toes and around either side of the foot. Can any of you guess where the words flip flop came from?

Student 1: Maybe from the sound that is made when you walk across a floor?

Professor: You're absolutely right! That modern term dates from the 1960s. Any guesses as to about how old the basic design is?

Student 2: I think in the middle of the twentieth century, America began importing something like today's flip flops from Japan.

Professor: That is correct. But actually they originated as early as the ancient Egyptians in 4000 BC. Archeologists have seen pictures of them in ancient murals. Another pair found in Europe was made of papyrus leaves and dates back approximately 1,500 years.

Student 3: Yeah, whenever you see historical movies of the Middle East, like those of Cleopatra, all the people are wearing them.

Professor: Yes, and ancient Greeks and Romans as well. Around the fifteenth century, the Masai of Africa made them out of rawhide. In India, they've been made from wood for hundreds of years. In China and Japan rice straw was used. And the natives of Mexico used the yucca plant.

Student 2: But nowadays they're mainly plastic, right?

Professor: Yes. As you mentioned earlier, after World War II, they caught on here in the postwar boom, and as they became adopted into American popular culture, the sandals began to sport the bright colors that dominated the 1950s design.

Student 1: And then there were all those beach and surfer movies with all the actors wearing them.

Professor: Once they became more acceptable, some people started wearing them for more formal occasions. Who knows the most famous brand?

Student 3: Aren't they the Brazilian ones, the Havaianas?

Professor: You're correct. Started in 1962, these quickly became some of the most popular in the world. Since 2010, more than 150 million pairs have been made every year. Flip-flops have come to dominate the casual footwear of women and men.

Student2: I did wear them for a while, but I twisted my ankle while wearing them.

Professor: You're not alone. They have no support and often wearers scrunch their toes to hold the sandals in place, resulting in tendonitis. Ankle sprains and even broken bones occur from stepping off a curb incorrectly. The ankle bends, but the flip flop neither holds on to nor supports it. Despite all these issues, flip flops do not have to be avoided completely. Many podiatrists, foot doctors, recommend avoiding the inexpensive, cheaply made ones and spending a little bit of extra money on sandals with thick-cushioned soles.

Student 1: So tell us the truth. Do you wear them?

Professor: Of course I do. Just not to class!

Track 22 [page 79]

9. Listen again to part of the passage. Then answer the question.

Professor: As I look around today, I see many of you are wearing flip flops even though you're not going to the beach or a swimming pool. I'm sure most of you have no idea about their evolution.

Narrator: What does the professor mean when she says this?

Professor: I see many of you are wearing flip flops even though you're not going to the beach or a swimming pool.

Questions 11-16

Track 23 [page 80]

Listen to a lecture in a legal studies class.

Professor: Remember last class we were discussing how important expert witnesses can be when presenting your case in the courtroom. Today I want to review with you the qualities lawyers look for in hiring an expert witness to take the stand. Although there are no specific requirements that all experts must meet, depending on the case and the subjects involved, lawyers selecting an expert look for the following criteria. First, it may seem obvious, but a lawyer needs to determine that he or she gets along with the expert. Second, the lawyer needs to verify that this witness is someone that the judge and, more importantly, the jury will understand, respect, like, and trust. If a jury of ordinary people cannot understand or believe the witness, this testimony is worthless.

Next, different fields of expertise have different educational requirements. In some cases, advanced degrees are mandatory. If you're trying to prove someone's medical condition, your witness must be a licensed medical doctor who is currently practicing. The more impressive the credentials, such as published articles, the more likely the jury will believe the testimony. On the other hand, if you are attempting to prove that a building was set on fire, a firefighter with many years of experience would suffice. If the expert works in a field for which state or federal licensing is required, obviously the expert should have the required license. Of course, if the witness has written something that is inconsistent with his or her expected testimony, there would be a lot of explaining to do, as you can assume that the other side will find out about it. In such cases, the lawyer would possibly be better off using an expert who had never written anything.

Some lawyers look for those witnesses who have a history as expert witnesses. Lawyers are understandably nervous about using a witness who may not understand the pressure involved in a cross-examination. Others prefer a fresh face who has rarely testified and is not likely to be regarded as a professional witness, one who testifies often. Juries may perceive this kind of witness as someone who testifies just for the money.

Speaking of money, experts can be expensive to hire. With that said, you can figure that an expert will charge slightly more than the typical amount he or she normally earns. You can be sure that this amount will be raised in the cross-examination. So, for example, if you have a dentist testifying who normally earns a hundred dollars an hour, and it is revealed that you are paying the dentist five hundred dollars an hour, how would you react if you were sitting on the jury? Would you probably conclude that this expert was being paid an extra four hundred dollars an hour in an effort to buy the testimony?

As I told you last class, experts play critically important roles in the courtroom. The more important of complex the matter, the more likely it is that one or more experts will be involved for each side.

Track 24 [page 81]

15. Listen again to part of the passage. Then answer the question.

Professor: So, for example, if you have a dentist testifying who normally a hundred dollars an hour, and it is revealed that you are paying the dentist five hundred dollars an hour, how would you react if you were sitting on the jury?

What does the professor mean when he says this?

Professor: How would you react if you were sitting on the jury?

Questions 17 through 22

Track 25 [page 82]

Listen to a discussion in a chemistry class.

Professor: Welcome to Organic Chemistry. Today we'll be talking about some of the basics of molecules. We'll see how molecules govern every aspect of our lives. For example, how do chemicals—of course made up of molecules—regulate our bodies? Why did your muscles ache after the Zumba class you took this morning? What is in the pill you took to get rid of the headache you had after studying all night for a final exam? Since I've asked you all to have your cards folded with your first names facing me, I'll be calling on you to answer some of my questions. Can you think of any other questions that examining molecules can answer? I see a hand up. Yes, Samantha.

Student 1: Of course. What happens to gasoline after I fill up my car?

Professor: Good question. Anyone else? Brandon?

Student2: Why does garlic smell the way it does?

Professor: Yup. Another? What about you, Ashley?

Student 3: I'm not sure, but, aren't there different molecular compositions to the clothes we wear? Like how is silk different from polyester?

Professor: Exactly. We'll find the answers to these questions and many many others that you have probably asked yourself as we study organic chemistry together this semester. Does anyone know what the definition of organic chemistry, say in contrast to other chemical disciplines, such as inorganic or physical chemistry?

Student 1: I remember, hopefully correctly from high school, that organic chemistry studies carbon and its compounds. Aren't these compounds called organic molecules?

Professor: That's correct. These organic molecules constitute the building blocks of life. Fats, sugars, proteins, and the nucleic acids are compounds in which the principal component is carbon. So are countless substances that we take for granted in everyday life. Back to your answer, Ashley. All the clothes that we wear are made up of organic materials, some of natural fibers, like what?

Student 2: Silk, as Ashley said, and cotton.

Professor: And artificial ones, like the polyester she also mentioned. Every day we use and are surrounded by products made of organic compounds, such as toothbrushes and shampoo as well as furniture, food, and cooking utensils. Consequently, organic chemical industries are among some of the largest in the world, such as…?

Student 1: Plastics and pharmaceuticals. You mentioned pills and furniture.

Student 3: Yeah, Someone mentioned gasoline, so petroleum refining, right?

Student 2: And you mentioned fats and sugars, so I'm guessing all the food producers.

Professor: You're all exactly right. Organic substances such as gasoline, medicines, and even pesticides have improved the quality of our lives. However, the uncontrolled disposal of organic chemicals has polluted the environment, causing deterioration of animal and plant life as well as injury and disease to humans. If we are to create useful molecules and learn to control their effects, we need knowledge of their properties and understanding of their behavior. We need to apply the principles of organic chemistry. Our first chapter, that I hope you've all read for today, will explain how the basic ideas of chemical structure and bonding apply to organic molecules. Most of it I'm sure was a review of the topics you covered in your general chemistry courses.

Track 26 [page 83]

Professor: Every day we use and are surrounded by products made of organic compounds such as toothbrushes and shampoo as well as furniture, food, and cooking utensils. Consequently, organic chemical industries are among some of the largest in the world, such as…?

What does the professor mean when he says this?

Professor: Organic chemical industries are among some of the largest in the world, such as…?

Questions 23 through 28

Track 27 [page 84]

Listen to a lecture in a dental hygiene class.

Professor: When I was going to school, I would be sent down to the principal's office for chewing gum in school. We were told that chewing gum was bad, that it caused cavities. And of course, no one liked to clean up gum that had been stuck under desks. Like chocolate and coffee, gum is now being rehabilitated. It turns out that sugar-free gum can actually prevent cavities in children. Instead of banning it, we should require children to chew it in school to promote their oral health.

The human mouth is host to many bacteria. The one that is primarily responsible for cavities is called streptococcus mutans. When the bacteria encounter sugar, acids are produced. Saliva, the fluids in your mouth, neutralizes acid, so teeth can handle some exposure. But large amounts of sugar, such as the amount found in a candy bar or a soda, overwhelm saliva. Prolonged exposure to that acid will damage the protective enamel on teeth. This process is called demineralization and eventually causes cavities.

Chewing gum of any kind increases saliva production, thereby helping to neutralize more acid. However, many gums are sweetened with sugar, which of course increases the acid level, canceling out the positive benefits. Replacing sugar in gum with xylitol, a naturally occurring sweetener found in fruits and vegetables that has fewer calories than regular sugar, fixes this problem.

More saliva and less acid seem to cause the teeth to remineralize, that means it actually reverses some cavities. But most important, chewing xylitol gum inhibits the growth of the strep bacteria, which are not able to metabolize the sweetener. Less infectious strains of bacteria slip off the teeth, and this positive xylitol effect lasts years. The gum seems to work best when it's chewed routinely just before children's adult teeth come in, at about ages 5 and 6.

We have known about this for a surprisingly long time. High quality randomized studies in Finland and Belize showed the benefits of chewing xylitol-sweetened gum. In Belize,

10-year-old children who chewed this type of gum decreased the risk of cavities by up to 70 percent, and a follow-up study showed that the benefit lasted up to five years. Studies in day care centers in Finland showed that xylitol chewing gum may also reduce ear infections in children by up to 40 percent.

So why haven't school systems or the government acted on this information? Perhaps school administrators do not know about the international data. Certainly, after a century of bubbles blown in class, it must be difficult for them to see chewing gum as a virtue instead of a vice. But they do need to come around.

In the United States alone more than 50 million hours of school are missed every year because of dental problems, not to mention those lost because of ear infections. There is an easy, cost-effective solution: having children chew gum with significant amounts of xylitol, which can usually be found in any corner store. The best way to ensure that all children take advantage of xylitol gum is to have them chew it in school, in kindergarten, and beyond. Ideally, they would chew three to five times a day for five minutes each time. Not only will it improve their health and school attendance but they might actually enjoy it.

Track 28 [page 85]

Listen again to part of the passage. Then answer the question.

Professor: When I was going to school, I would be sent down to the principal's office for chewing gum in school. We were told that chewing gum was bad, that it caused cavities. And of course, no one liked to clean up gum that had been stuck under desks.

Why does the professor say this?

Professor: And of course, no one liked to clean up gum that had been stuck under desks.

Questions 29 through 34

Track 29 [page 86]

Listen to a lecture in a linguistics class.

Professor: It's important to see the evolution of the letters in our alphabet. I'll be referring to this alphabet as the basic Latin alphabet. The original alphabet was developed by a Semitic people living in or near Egypt. They based it on the idea developed by the Egyptians, but used their own specific symbols. It was quickly adopted by their neighbors and relatives to the east and north, the

Canaanites, the Hebrews, and the Phoenicians. The Phoenicians spread their alphabet to other people of the Near East and Asia Minor, as well as to the Arabs, the Greeks, and Etruscans, and as far west as present day Spain. The earliest certain ancestor of our letter A is *aleph*, the first letter of the Phoenician alphabet. The origins of aleph may have been a pictogram of an ox head in Egyptian hieroglyphs. In 1600 B.C., the Phoenician letter had a linear form that served as the base for some later forms. Its name must have corresponded closely to the Hebrew or Arabic *aleph*. When the ancient Greeks adopted the alphabet, they gave it the similar name of *alpha*. In the earliest Greek writing, dating to the eighth century BC, the letter rests upon its side, but in the Greek alphabet of later times, it generally resembles the modern capital letter although many local varieties can be distinguished by the shortening of one leg or by the angle at which the cross line occurs.

The Etruscans brought the Greek alphabet to their civilization in the Italian Peninsula and left the letter unchanged. The Romans later adopted the Etruscan alphabet to write the Latin language, and the resulting letter was preserved in the Latin alphabet used to write many languages, including English.

The letter has two lower-case, or miniscule, forms. The form used in most current handwriting consists of a circle and vertical stroke (ɑ) This slowly developed from the fifth-century form resembling the Greek letter *tau* in the hands of Irish and English writers. Most printed materials use a form consisting of a loop with an arc over it (a). Both derive from the capital, or majuscule form. In Greek handwriting, it was common to join the left leg and horizontal stroke into a single loop (ɑ). Many fonts then made the right leg vertical, resulting in the handwritten form today.

In English, the letter A currently represents six different vowel sounds. The most common is the *ay* sound in the word *pay* and the *eh* sound in the word *pad*. The letter A is the third most commonly used letter in English, and the second most common in Spanish and French. A is often used to denote something or someone of a better of more prestigious quality of status. An A is the best grade used in school. Some schools even use A+ to signify work of the highest quality. We also use the letter A in terms such as A-list celebrities, meaning the most well-known or best ones. Triple A rating is the best bond

rating given to investments. Such associations can have a motivating effect as exposure to the letter A has been found to improve performance when compared to other letters.

Speaking

Track 30 [page 90]

1. You will hear a question about a familiar topic. Listen to the question, and then prepare a response. You will have 15 seconds to prepare a response and 45 seconds to speak. You can take notes on the main points of a response.

   If you won a million dollars, what would you do with the money? Use specific examples and details in your response.

Track 31 [page 91]

2. You will be asked your opinion about a familiar topic. Listen to the question, and then prepare your response. You will have 15 seconds to prepare a response and 45 seconds to speak. You can take notes on the main points of a response.

   Can you think of a time when it would be OK to lie? When would that be? Use reasons and details to support your response.

Track 32 [page 92]

3. You will read a short passage and then listen to a conversation about the same topic. You will then answer a question about about them. You will have 45 seconds to read the passage. You can take notes on the main points of the reading passage.

Listen to two students talking.

Man: Did you know we can have free dental checkups done at the campus dental clinic?

Woman: No. I hadn't heard that. How did you find out?

Man: There was a notice that just went up, and one of the dental hygiene students in my math class made an announcement about it. They're looking for volunteers. Seems they need to find a certain number of patients to practice on in order to pass their clinic class.

Woman: Would you want a student working on your teeth?

Man: Someone made a joke about it when she asked, so she explained that a registered dentist is always in the clinic and walks around checking every student and patient.

Woman: Well, I guess the students are just cleaning your teeth, right? They're not doing procedures like filling cavities or pulling teeth, are they?

Man: No, no. Just cleaning the teeth and checking for any problems.

Woman: So are you going to do it?

Man: I haven't decided yet. It's free and I would be helping my classmate, but I do have a regular dentist that I've been going to for about five years. I'm planning on seeing him for my regular checkup when I'm home next.

Woman: I'm with you. I'd rather have someone already licensed work on my teeth.

Now answer the following question:

The students express their opinions about going to the Campus Dental Clinic. State their opinions and explain the resaons they give for holding those opinions.

Track 33 [page 94]

4. You will read a short passage and then listen to a conversation about the same topic. You will then answer a question about about them. You will have 45 seconds to read the passage. You can take notes on the main points of the reading passage.

Listen to the passage.

Professor: Allie, can you stay a few minutes after class?

Student: Of course. Is there a problem?

Professor: No, I just want to have a word with you. You have in your hand that first paper I just returned today. I know you haven't had a chance to look it over. After you do, I suggest you go to the writing center with it.

Student: Oh, the one in Ricker Hall?

Professor: Have you ever been?

Student: No, I thought it was for students who really couldn't write well, but I guess maybe I'm in that category. Do I just show up?

Professor: It's for everyone, and everyone's writing can improve. It's free, and you can make an appointment in person, on the phone, or by email. I'd like you to take the paper with you and have one of the tutors there go over it with you.

Student: Is it my grammar or spelling or what?

Professor: That's part of it, but the writing center does not do line editing for those kinds of errors. What they do is take a look at my comments in those areas and recognize the patterns of errors. For example, I recall I wrote on your paper that you made several errors with dangling modifiers. They'll be able to give you some exercises for that.

Student: Yeah, I know I have some grammar problems. What else?

Professor: What I'd really like them to help you with has to do with organization. Your thesis statement needs to be more precise because that affects the whole paper. Once that is better crafted, you'll be better able to find evidence and make each paragraph related to the thesis. You'll see also that the introduction needs to have more background.

Student: Ouch.

Professor: Hey, it's just the first paper, and on a positive note, many of your ideas are very interesting, and the evidence you use from the readings supports your claims very nicely.

Student: Thanks. I was starting to feel totally depressed.

Professor: That's certainly not my intention. I see lots of potential, and we're really lucky to have such an exceptional writing center on campus. Once you go, I'd like you to rewrite the paper, by next week if possible. You should rewrite it before we start the next one.

Student: I'll go right now and make an appointment.

Now answer the following question:

How do the professor and student feel about using the College Writing Center?

Track 34 [page 96]

5. You will listen to part of a lecture. You can take notes on the main points of the listening passage.

Woman: Are you going to submit your thesis poster for the conference?

Man: I wasn't going to until the professor told us on Monday that there would be funding for three students from our class.

Woman: Yeah, and it's in San Diego. I've always wanted to go there.

Man: The odds aren't bad. There are only 12 students in the seminar.

Woman: My problem is the deadline. He wants them next Friday. The seminar deadline is a month after that, so I haven't even started it.

Man: Me neither. I know what you mean. When he told us earlier in the semester about the conference and the student poster part, I barely paid attention. I knew I didn't have money to go to San Diego. Now suddenly there's money.

Woman: Well, at least we finished the research last semester. And he's spent several classes on poster design, and he's given us the template to use.

Man:	Do you wanna go over to the design lab with me at about 4? The lab assistant is there then, and he can help us.
Woman:	What time is it now? Noon. Ok. I'll be in the library making a rough sketch. We can't go to the lab empty handed.
Man:	If you apply, it'll inspire me. It would be so much fun to go, all expenses paid.
Woman:	Let alone how good it will look on your résumé that you presented at a national conference!

Now answer the following question:

How do the students feel about submitting their posters?

Track 35 [page 97]

6. Listen to part of a lecture. You can take notes on the main points of the listening passage.

Professor: Textile fragment analysis from the excavation of a fifth century Mayan tomb, in the Central American country of Honduras, has recently revealed high quality fabrics, which strongly suggests that the Mayans were highly skilled spinners and weavers. Also inside the tomb the remains of a woman of high status who was buried during the fifth century were found. Tiny fragments of 49 textile samples were brought back to a U.S. laboratory for analysis. Special microscopes examined each specimen for yarn structure, fabric structure, and the finish. Due to the climate of the warm and humid tropics, the discovery of these specimens is remarkable.

The analysis found different threads made from cotton, various grass forms, and all kinds of plant fibers. In the ancient Mayan tomb, there were as many as 25 layers of fabrics on a platform covering pottery. All of them had a different fabric structure, color, and yarn size. It is likely that the tomb was reopened several times, and additional layers of textiles were laid there years after the woman's death. One of the fabrics had an especially high thread count of 100 yards per inch, which is considered high for textiles even nowadays. In order to fashion such exceptional textiles, the Mayans used many different kinds of sophisticated weaving tools. No evidence of such tools in the same period have been found anywhere else. The discovery from the tomb speaks to the technology the Mayans had at the time for spinning and weaving very fine fabrics.

Now answer the following question:

How does the professor explain the skill level of ancient Mayans?

Writing 2

Track 36 [page 101]

Listen to part of a lecture in a hospitality class.

Professor: While cruise companies advertise extensively on television and online, as future travel agents, you should carefully consider whether or not to recommend a cruise to a client. Due to some well-publicized problems at sea, prices for cruises are at an all-time low. But before you let the price be the deciding factor, consider some of the negatives of cruising.

First of all, the all-inclusive price pays for usually a small interior room. A balcony room is an expensive upgrade. Also, land tours are not part of the deal, nor are expensive on-board spa treatments.

Because there are so many people on board in a confined, albeit large space, travelers may have to put up with noisy neighbors who disregard the no-smoking signs or party all night long. The constant waiting in line for meals and being part of a big group may not be everyone's cup of tea. Loudspeaker announcements seem neverending.

Although travelers on cruises visit many places, there's no option to stay longer at any port that seems exciting, nor is there a chance to meet locals, or sample the cuisine.

Sometimes rough seas make even hearty travelers seasick, so these cruisers cannot enjoy all the onboard activities, meals, and entertainment.

Now answer the following question:

How does the information in the listening passage cast doubt on the information presented in the reading passage?

Answer Key

Practice Test 1

Reading 1

1.	A	5.	B	8.	A	11.	A
2.	C	6.	D	9.	C	12.	A
3.	B	7.	B	10.	D	13.	2, 3, 6
4.	D						

Reading 2

14.	A	18.	A	21.	B	24.	A
15.	C	19.	B	22.	C	25.	C
16.	D	20.	D	23.	B	26.	1, 3, 6
17.	B						

Reading 3

27.	D	31.	B	34.	A	37.	D
28.	A	32.	C	35.	D	38.	B
29.	A	33.	C	36.	B	39.	1, 5, 6
30.	C						

Practice Test 1 – Listening

1.	D	8.	C	15.	C	22.	C
2.	A, C	9.	D	16.	A	23.	B
3.	A	10.	D	17.	D	24.	B
4.	B	11.	B	18.	B	25.	B, C
5.	C	12.	D	19.	C, D, E		
6.	C	13.	C	20.	C		
7.	A, C	14.	A, B	21.	B		

26. Cheaper models: Used a drip pan that was placed under the box

More expensive models: Used spigots for draining ice water from a catch pan

Refrigeration models: Used electricity instead of ice

27. A

28. 2, 4, 1, 3

29. C

30. A

31. B, C

32. 1. YES;   2. NO;   3. YES;   4. NO

33. A

34. C

Practice Test 2

Reading 1

1.	A	4.	B	7.	C	10.	A
2.	C	5.	A	8.	C	11.	B
3.	C	6.	C	9.	A	12.	2, 4, 6

Reading 2

13.	A	17.	C	20.	B	23.	D
14.	B	18.	C	21.	D	24.	A
15.	C	19.	D	22.	C	25.	1, 3, 6
16.	A						

Reading 3

26.	A	29.	D	31.	B	33.	C
27.	D	30.	C	32.	A	34.	C
28.	B						

35. Organic fertilizer: Meal from cotton kernels; Mulch: By-product from cotton ginning; Housing insulation: Recycled old jeans

36. Today: Medical supplies, Mulch, Navy ship fire hoses, Fish food

   Future: Housing insulation, Soil erosion reduction, Cleaning oil spills

Practice Test 2 – Listening

1.	D	3.	B	5.	B	7.	B, C, D
2.	A, D	4.	A, B, D	6.	D		

8. Masai of Africa: Rawhide; India: Wood; Europe: Papyrus leaves

9.	B	16.	B, D	23.	B	30.	C, D
10.	B, C	17.	C	24.	C	31.	D
11.	D	18.	A, B	25.	4, 3, 2, 1	32.	A, C
12.	B	19.	C	26.	A, B, C	33.	D
13.	D	20.	C	27.	C	34.	B, D
14.	B	21.	C	28.	C		
15.	A	22.	C	29.	B		

Sample Answers

Practice Test 1

Speaking

Question 1

My most treasured possession is my grandmother's sewing box. Although my grandmother died several years ago, every time I open it up, I think of her. It still has her different colored threads, needles, pins, scissors, and tape measure. She was a talented seamstress. I'm not, but I believe that by using all of her things, some of her talent is passing through to me. When I was younger, I used to sit and watch her sew. She would thread a needle for me and let me practice sewing on pieces of extra cloth she kept in the box just for me. I loved visiting her because I knew she would let me sew and teach me something new each time I saw her. The sewing box is big, pink, and old…kind of like how I remember my grandmother. Although I could buy something more stylish, I know I'll keep it forever.

Question 2

There are some good reasons to attend a large university just as there are some good reasons to attend a small one. Personally, I would rather attend a large one although I know there are many people who don't feel that way. First of all, I like the idea of having many students around me. If I were at a small school, I think I would feel that very quickly I would know everyone and would want to meet new people. I'm not saying I need tons of friends, just that I would enjoy meeting many people. I went to a small high school and wished I had gone to a larger one. Second, at a large school there would be a wide variety of courses I could take. By having the ability to take many different courses my first year, I would be able to decide what I then want to major in. At a smaller school I wouldn't have such a variety.

Question 3

The man and the woman feel very differently about staying in the hotel. The man, on the one hand, expresses many advantages. The hotel has air conditioning, cable TV, one bathroom for two students, and an indoor pool. Obviously the dorm has none of those things. Instead of having to change and launder his own sheets, the hotel does it for him. His teachers have been really considerate about the fact that he and others are not on campus. One put books on reserve in the library. Another gave out lecture notes from previous classes, and another invited those staying in the hotel to his house for dinner.

On the other hand, the woman feels really stuck staying in the hotel. She admits the hotel is nicer than the dorm, but she lists many disadvantages in staying here. She can't go back to her room between classes like she could when she's in the dorm. Because of the fire, they all had to leave quickly, so she doesn't have most of her books or clothes. She's had to wear the same sweater for three days in a row. She's worried about her grades, especially because she has a big chemistry test this week and doesn't have her notes. She's really hoping she can get back into the dorm soon so that she can get some of her stuff.

Question 4

The reading passage discusses parent/child sleeping arrangements. They vary around the world. Should young children sleep with their parents or in a separate room? The passage then mentions that in the United States usually children do not sleep with their parents, whereas in Japan it's different. In Japan usually no one, including children, ever sleeps alone. About half of Japanese children sleep in the same bed as their mother or father, and others sleep with brothers or sisters.

The listening passage points out that Americans seem to be obsessed with whether or not children should sleep with parents and that those from other cultures where this practice is commonplace may find humor in the debate. He explains that the American pressure NOT to sleep with children has many sources, such as relatives, other parents, and even the children's doctors who fear that if a child is in bed with a parent, the parent may roll over, killing the baby. In America, many believe that children need to learn, even as infants, how to be self-sufficient. Sleeping with a parent would somehow prevent children from being independent.

However, the listening passage adds that there is now a small but growing movement in the United States that favors parents and children co-sleeping, pointing to Japan where parents and children have slept together for hundreds of years. A university doctor conducted some cross-cultural studies and found no connection between sleeping alone as babies and being able to develop a sense of independence.

Question 5

It's really interesting that the well-known CAT scan machine was funded by the Beatles, the famous rock-and-roll band. Most people don't know that even though most people are familiar with this machine. The first time the machine was used was in England in 1971 when it took a brain scan. It uses computer-processed X-rays that produce slices of specific body areas.

The CAT scan images are far superior to traditional X-rays that had been commonly used until 1971, and it can detect disease much earlier. The number of CAT scan procedures done in the U.S. has increased dramatically since 1980 because of improvements in technology and the speed of the scan. Initially the machines cost more, but since more have been produced, the cost has decreased. This machine earned the Nobel Prize in Medicine.

Question 6

The woman's problem is that she needs to take the one-credit human service course before she does her externship, but if she takes it, she'll have 19 credits, and she will have to pay for the extra credit. A full load is 15 credits, but they can take 18 for no additional charge. Because she had to take a no credit developmental math course, she is a course behind.

The students discuss two possible solutions to her problem. The man suggests that she could ask the professor if she could audit the course, that is take the course without paying. Since the student doesn't need the credit to graduate, the professor might let her do this. She needs to know what is covered in the course.

The other option is to take the extra three credits she needs in the semester while they're doing the externship. She's afraid that she'll be too busy since she'll have to travel to a site plus spend 100 hours there.

I think she should first ask the teacher if she can audit the course. It might be a problem if the teacher needs a certain number of registered students in order to have the course run. Then the professor would have to say no. But if that's not a problem, and the professor agrees, she should audit it. I fear that overextending herself while doing the externship is not a good idea.

Writing

Question 1

The reading passage asserts that the main reason for the decrease in the number of bees around the world is the increase in using cell phones. When cell phones are used near hives, radiation is generated, and as a result, the bees do not return to the hives. These results were proven in two different European university studies. The conclusion of the studies suggests that the microwaves emitted from mobile phone are what affect the navigational skills of the bees, causing their inability to return to their hives. Although initially the rapid bee decrease was inexplicable, the cell phone magnetism explains the occurrence.

In contrast, the listening passage asserts that there is no one cause for the decline in the bee population but that the major reason is pesticides. Although cell phones, as well as global warming, contribute to the problem, they are not the major reason. The pesticides affect the bees' central nervous system and cause death. There are laws in place limiting the use of pesticides, but even low doses impact the bees' memory and the ability to return home to the hives.

Question 2

There are many talents that I wish I had that I don't have, but if I had to pick only one it would be the ability to draw. I've always had an interest in the arts, and I believe I have a good sense of design. I knit and have studied calligraphy and have dabbled in painting some abstract pieces, but I'm not able to draw realistically. I wish I were an artist.

Perhaps I'm imagining that this talent would do more for me than it could. For some reason, I believe drawing would be a stress reliever. Whenever I would be anxious or under stress of any kind, I picture myself taking out a box of colored pencils or tubes of paint and being able to block out any negative thoughts or anxieties by simply drawing. I envision myself totally immersed in creating a picture, thinking only about perspective or shading or color choice.

What else could this talent do for me? Maybe I would be so talented that I could be a professional artist and make my living from my artwork. How romantic it would be to paint in an artist's studio, surrounded by other talented artists! I close my eyes, and I'm a French Impressionist living in Paris in the 1800s. The next moment I'm sharing a studio with Picasso in Spain in the twentieth century. Or maybe it's today, and I'm living on Cape Cod and painting the seascapes. Better yet, I'm living in Soho in New York City, getting ready for my upcoming gallery show.

I do not believe that I do not need to be famous in order to appreciate this talent. Like any gift, the ability to draw should be appreciated for its own sake, as a means to make my current life even more fulfilling.

Practice Test 2

Speaking

Question 1

Wow! A million dollars. There are so many things I could do with a million dollars. First of all, I would buy a car. It's really difficult taking a bus to work and school, and that would save me so much time and energy.

Next, I would take a vacation with my parents. I've always wanted to go on a cruise with them. I know there are so many activities on cruise ships that they would find things to do, and so would I. I would take one that stopped in lots of countries we haven't been to.

I know I would still have lots of money after that. I would put a big chunk of it in the bank for my future, but would still think about charity. There are so many deserving organizations and needy people around the world. I would make sure the money is really going where it says it is, not like the author of "Three Cups of Tea" who used much of the money donated on himself.

Question 2

Is it ever OK to lie? Hmm. Let me think about that. In theory probably not because from experience you will probably get caught in a lie, but I can think of two situations where it's probably better to do so.

Imagine your best friend has just had her hair cut. You don't think it looks good and she asks, "Do you like my hair better this way?" It would just be painful for you to say, "Oh, it looked better before." If she had asked you BEFORE she cut it, "Do you think I should cut my hair?" then you can be honest. But once it's cut, it's too late and it would just make her feel bad.

Another time I believe it's OK to lie is dealing with your parents. Let's say you've left home to go to school thousands of miles away, and you're homesick. Your parents call and ask, "How's everything?" Are you really going to say, "I'm miserable." when you know how sad it will make them, and there's nothing they can do about it?

Question 3

Dental hygiene students are conducting free dental checkups, including teeth cleaning, X-rays, and scaling on campus for students, and the two students are discussing whether they would want a student to clean their teeth. The man mentions that although the students are doing the cleaning, there is always a dentist in the clinic who walks around to make sure everything is being done correctly. The student clinicians will not be doing any procedures, such as filling cavities or pulling teeth. These dental hygiene students have had a year of coursework and have completed the state requirements in order to work on patients.

The man tells the woman that a student made an announcement about the checkups in his math class. Each dental hygiene student needs to find a certain number of volunteers. Although the man appreciates that the checkup would be free and that he would be helping a classmate who needs a patient to practice on in order to pass the clinic class, he does have a regular dentist he's been seeing for five years at home. He was planning on going to see his dentist for a regular checkup when he goes home next.

The woman agrees and adds she'd prefer to have someone licensed to do work on her teeth.

Question 4

Initially when the professor suggests that the student go to the writing center, she is somewhat taken aback. She had thought it was for students who couldn't write well, and she obviously thought she wasn't one of them. The professor then explains that the writing center is for everyone, and that everyone's writing can improve.

She does recognize that she has some problems with grammar, and the professor points out that she'll be able to get some help with grammar at the center. They won't make corrections, but they'll give her some exercises in areas of weakness.

The professor wants her to go before he gives the next paper assignment so that she has a better grasp on thesis statements and relating her paragraphs to the thesis. He tells her that it's free, and it's really easy to make an appointment. You can do it in person, by phone, or on the computer. He also adds that it's a really wonderful writing center, and that the college is lucky to have such a good one.

She tells him that she will go and work on her paper in order to rewrite it by next week.

Question 5

Two students are discussing submitting their thesis posters for an upcoming conference in San Diego. The professor told them on Monday that three students out of the 12 in their class will be funded to attend. The posters need to be submitted by Friday. The deadline for the course is a month after that. Since the students had thought there would not be funding available for the conference when the professor first mentioned it, they hadn't even started the posters, knowing they didn't have the money to attend.

Now that there's a good chance they could get funded, they're discussing trying to get the posters done by Friday. The research for the poster design was completed last semester, so what's left is actually designing the poster. The professor has given them a template for how to design the poster and has spent several classes discussing how to do it.

The man suggests they go over to the design lab that afternoon because there's a lab assistant there who can help them. The woman agrees, saying she'll spend about four hours in the library making some sketches. She doesn't want to go empty handed to the lab. The man thinks it would be fun if they both got to go, and the woman mentions how good it would look on their résumés that they presented at a national conference.

Question 6

Excavations of Mayan weaving from the fifth century in Honduras showed that the Mayans were skilled spinners and weavers. Researchers were able to determine this fact by analyzing textiles found in a tomb there. These textiles were brought back to the United States and special equipment examined the fabrics. What was interesting was that in one woman's tomb there were 25 layers of fabric, all of which had a different structure. One of the fabrics had a thread count of over 100 yards per inch, which is high for even modern day textiles. Considering what kinds of tools these ancient spinners had at their disposal, it's truly remarkable. However, certain tools were found in the area. Tools dating from this era at this level of sophistication have not been found elsewhere. This fact speaks to the high skill level of fifth century Mayan weavers.

Writing

Question 1

The reading passage describes the many benefits of taking a cruise. First the price is all-inclusive, so the meals, room, and entertainment are paid in advance in one amount. When everything is totaled, this vacation is typically cheaper than traveling on land. Because there are so many people on board, it is easy to meet others. Cruise ships stop at many ports, so cruising is a great way to visit numerous locations in a short amount of time. Lastly, due to the large number of onboard activities, everyone can find something enjoyable to do.

On the other hand, the listening passage enumerates the disadvantages of cruising. The all-inclusive price covers only a small interior room. Upgrades to a balcony room and other amenities are expensive. Traveling with so many people in a closed environment can be noisy, disruptive, and not to everyone's liking. If someone wants to stay longer at a site, meet locals, or sample the cuisine, it's not possible. Lastly, the weather may dampen the whole trip. Rough seas, producing seasickness, may make enjoying the many amenities impossible.

Question 2

Some people claim that all university courses should be taught online. Others disagree. Having had experience with online coursework, I believe that a combination of courses in the classroom coupled with online courses when necessary is the best scenario.

First, I recognize that there are those who propose online coursework only. For students in remote areas who perhaps cannot travel to universities or cannot afford to, studying online affords them an opportunity previously unavailable. In addition, some people who need to work and cannot be full-time students will find online learning an exciting possibility. For those who are ill or unable to travel, online learning serves a valuable purpose. I have to admit it was more comfortable to take my final exam in my pajamas lying on my bed.

However, having experienced online learning, I have several objections. I took an online course last semester. Although the professor provided insightful assignments, and we were able to communicate online with classmates, I found the course not as enjoyable or beneficial as classroom learning. I could email the professor a question, but the reply sometimes took a day or two. When the response came, I sometimes felt the professor hadn't really understood what I was asking. If we had been face to face I could have explained myself better and received instant feedback. The interaction with classmates wasn't in real time either. I know some online coursework affords that possibility, but since our classmates were all over the world, we posted our comments. Those interchanges were never as rich and thought-provoking as in-class discussions.

In conclusion, I acknowledge that there are circumstances where online learning is both a necessity and an opportunity. Nevertheless, if universities cease to be what they are today, a place where students and faculty exchange ideas, fostering learning and development, it will be a very sad day indeed.

 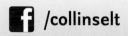

 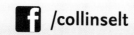

Collins Connect

Accessing the Online TOEFL® Tests and Training Module

The *Practice Test Pack for the TOEFL® Test* provides you with all the tools you need to succeed on the test.

An important part of your preparation for the TOEFL® iBT is the online component of the pack which you will find on **Collins Connect**.
This includes:

- Four complete TOEFL® tests
- An interactive training module

To access the online tests and training module go to www.connect.collins.co.uk/ELT and follow the instructions.

The access code is

5837TFL

If you need any help with registering on Collins Connect, please contact us on

education.support@harpercollins.co.uk